OCCASIONAL
P A P E R

T0169289

Rebuilding Housing Along the Mississippi Coast

Ideas for Ensuring an Adequate Supply of Affordable Housing

Mark A. Bernstein, Julie Kim, Paul Sorensen,

Mark Hanson, Adrian Overton, Scott Hiromoto

RAND GULF STATES POLICY INSTITUTE

The research described in this report results from the RAND Corporation's continuing program of self-initiated research. Support for such research is provided, in part, by donors and by the independent research development provisions of RAND's contracts for the operation of its U.S. Department of Defense federally funded research and development centers. This research was conducted under the auspices of the Environment, Energy, and Economic Development Program (EEED) within RAND Infrastructure, Safety, and Environment (ISE). This report is being released jointly by EEED and by the RAND Gulf States Policy Institute (RGSPI).

Library of Congress Cataloging-in-Publication Data

Rebuilding housing along the Mississippi Coast : ideas for ensuring an adequate supply of affordable housing /
    Mark A. Bernstein ... [et al.].
        p. cm.
    "OP-162."
    Includes bibliographical references.
    ISBN 0-8330-3949-0 (pbk. : alk. paper)
    1. Low-income housing—Government policy—Mississippi—Delta (Region) 2. Hurricane Katrina, 2005.
I. Bernstein, Mark (Mark A.)

HD7287.96.M72D457 2006
363.509762'1—dc22
                                                                                                                2006013366

The RAND Corporation is a nonprofit research organization providing objective analysis and effective solutions that address the challenges facing the public and private sectors around the world. RAND's publications do not necessarily reflect the opinions of its research clients and sponsors.

RAND® is a registered trademark.

Published 2006 by the RAND Corporation
1776 Main Street, P.O. Box 2138, Santa Monica, CA 90407-2138
1200 South Hayes Street, Arlington, VA 22202-5050
4570 Fifth Avenue, Suite 600, Pittsburgh, PA 15213-2612
RAND URL: http://www.rand.org/
To order RAND documents or to obtain additional information, contact
Distribution Services: Telephone: (310) 451-7002;
Fax: (310) 451-6915; Email: order@rand.org

Preface

Soon after Hurricane Katrina devastated the Gulf Coast of Mississippi, Governor Haley Barbour formed a commission to develop recommendations for rebuilding southern Mississippi. The mission for the Governor's Commission on Recovery, Rebuilding, Renewal was to establish a broad vision for rebuilding and simultaneously improving the areas affected by the hurricane. The Commission produced a final report that was delivered to the governor on December 31, 2005, and released to the public in mid-January. The report provided local leaders with access to (1) ideas and information to help them envision what their region could look five, ten, twenty, or even thirty years from now; and (2) strategies and policy options to support their efforts.

This report, which follows the release of the Commission's final report, reviews work performed by the RAND Corporation in support of the Commission's Affordable Housing Subcommittee. Specifically, it considers affordable-housing policy and implementation options that have potential application for long-term reconstruction decisions in the wake of natural disasters, such as those currently faced by the state of Mississippi following Hurricane Katrina. The report should be of interest to federal, state, and local policymakers, as well as to the private sector.

This research was conducted under the auspices of the Environment, Energy, and Economic Development Program (EEED) within RAND Infrastructure, Safety, and Environment (ISE). The mission of RAND Infrastructure, Safety, and Environment is to improve the development, operation, use, and protection of society's essential physical assets and natural resources and to enhance the related social assets of safety and security of individuals in transit and in their workplaces and communities. The EEED research portfolio addresses environmental quality and regulation, energy resources and systems, water resources and systems, climate, natural hazards and disasters, and economic development—both domestically and internationally. EEED research is conducted for government, foundations, and the private sector.

This report is being released jointly by EEED and by the RAND Gulf States Policy Institute (RGSPI). This paper results from the RAND Corporation's continuing program of self-initiated research. Support for such research is provided, in part, by donors and by the independent research and development provisions of RAND's contracts for the operation of its U.S. Department of Defense federally funded research and development centers.

Questions or comments about this report should be sent to the project co-leaders, Mark Bernstein (Mark_Bernstein@rand.org) and Julie Kim (Julie_Kim@rand.org). Information about the Environment, Energy, and Economic Development Program is available online (http://www.rand.org/ise/environ). Inquiries about EEED projects should be sent to the following address:

Michael Toman, Director
Environment, Energy, and Economic Development Program, ISE
RAND Corporation
1200 South Hayes Street
Arlington, VA 22202-5050
703-413-1100, x5189
Michael_Toman@rand.org

The RAND Gulf States Policy Institute

The RAND Gulf States Policy Institute is a collaboration among RAND and seven Gulf universities (Jackson State University, Tulane University, Tuskegee University, University of New Orleans, University of South Alabama, University of Southern Mississippi, and Xavier University) to develop a long-term vision and strategy to help build a better future for Louisiana, Mississippi, and Alabama in the wake of Hurricanes Katrina and Rita. The Institute's mission is to benefit the Gulf States region by providing officials in the government, nonprofit, and private sectors with the highest quality of analysis to help them not just to rebuild what the hurricanes destroyed, but to build a better and more prosperous future.

RGSPI is housed at the RAND Corporation, an international nonprofit research organization with a reputation for rigorous and objective analysis and effective solutions.

For additional information about the RAND Gulf States Policy Institute, contact its director:

George Penick
RAND Gulf States Policy Institute
P.O. Box 3788
Jackson, MS 39207
601-797-2499
George_Penick@rand.org

A profile of the RGSPI can be found at http://www.rand.org/about/katrina.html. More information about RAND is available on our Web site (http://www.rand.org).

Contents

Figures

Tables

Summary

Hurricane Katrina made landfall on August 29, 2005, near the Mississippi-Louisiana border, causing extensive damage along coastal Mississippi as well as in the neighboring states of Louisiana, Texas, and Alabama. Federal disaster declarations in the wake of Hurricane Katrina covered about 90,000 square miles. Mississippi took the brunt of the storm, with winds of up to 125 miles per hour and a storm surge that rose to more than 30 feet. More than 134,000 homes sustained some damage and at least 65,000 were completely destroyed. To date, more than a million households have received federal assistance, and countless agencies, organizations, and volunteers have responded to assist affected communities and individuals. More than 50,000 Mississippians from more than 18,000 households are living in trailers, while others live in hotel rooms scattered across 44 states and the District of Columbia. As in New Orleans, the challenge of recovering from Hurricane Katrina has been exacerbated by the fact that some of the poorest communities were also some of the hardest hit. Within Mississippi, many of the devastated areas are located in the six heavily populated counties closest to the coast, which are characterized by relatively high levels of poverty and relatively low levels of home ownership. To make matters worse, a substantial share of the homes in these areas that were exposed to high winds, flooding, and the coastal surge were built before 1980 and thus did not adhere to current, more-stringent building safety codes.

In October 2005, RAND Corporation researchers traveled to Mississippi to work with the Governor's Commission on Recovery, Rebuilding, Renewal and, more specifically, to assist the Affordable Housing Subcommittee of the Infrastructure Issues Committee. During the engagement, RAND researchers provided support in identifying and developing a list of policy and implementation options that could help local communities address affordable-housing issues in their rebuilding efforts. In developing this list of options, RAND researchers considered the following important questions:

- How is "affordable housing" defined, and what are some of the general affordable-housing issues faced by different regions in the United States? What are the critical challenges in providing affordable housing and what strategies are available to deal with these challenges?
- How have affordable-housing issues been addressed in the wake of other natural disasters in the United States? What lessons have we learned and what best practices can we take away from previous natural disaster experiences?

- What are the extent and scope of damage sustained by Mississippi relative to affordable housing? What types of affordable-housing needs should the state of Mississippi consider addressing during the rebuilding process, and at what scale?
- What affordable-housing policy options seem best suited to Mississippi's current needs?

RAND's analysis of these four questions is outlined in the sections below.

Critical Challenges in Providing Affordable Housing

Housing is typically considered "affordable" when a family does not need to spend more than 30 percent of its income on rent or on mortgage payments, insurance, and property taxes (Feldman, 2002), and when the housing is physically adequate and not overcrowded. By this definition, finding affordable housing is not a problem limited to the poor, and shortages of affordable housing at one income level can ripple upward to affect other income groups as well. For example, when lower-income families must live in homes or apartments that are beyond their means, it reduces the supply of housing for the next higher income group. This forces families in the next group to pay more for housing than they otherwise would, resulting in a domino effect that can extend through multiple levels of the available housing stock. Another common difficulty, one that occurs most frequently in suburban locations, arises where zoning codes limit the variety of housing types that can be built within a community. Because of this limitation, moderate-wage earners such as retail employees or blue-collar workers cannot find affordable housing within the community and must therefore either commute long distances or pay more for housing than they can afford. With such considerations in mind, we assume in this report that a key goal for Gulf Coast communities will be to ensure not only that there is an adequate supply of affordable housing across multiple income levels, but also that the affordable housing is located within a reasonable distance of suitable employment opportunities.

To put the affordable-housing challenge in Mississippi into a broader context, it is useful to note that, as of 2003, 7.5 million households nationwide were "severely burdened" by their housing costs. In more specific terms, this refers to households that must spend more than half of their income on rent or mortgage payments. In addition, estimates suggest that the supply of affordable housing within the United States is at least 1.6 million units short of what is needed (U.S. Department of Commerce, 2003).

This affordable-housing gap persists despite the variety of programs and subsidies put in place by federal and state governments. This gap exists in part because many government housing policies are aimed at home ownership, and people with the greatest needs often cannot afford to buy a home even with assistance. Another factor is that many of the projects developed through low-income housing tax credits still need other subsidies in order to become affordable for the lowest-income populations.

The literature we reviewed during the background-research phase of this study describes some strategies for reducing the affordable-housing gap in the United States. These strategies include the following:

- *Education.* Educating people on financial and housing options can improve their ability to find high-quality, affordable housing.
- *Lowering housing costs.* Lowering the costs by reducing fees, changing codes and zoning ordinances to allow for new technologies and housing styles to be introduced, reducing mortgage and insurance costs, providing additional finance options, and fostering public-private partnerships are strategies that provide more opportunities for families to find affordable housing.
- *Increasing the building and design standards for affordable housing.* Much of the affordable housing stock is also in disrepair and expensive to maintain. By applying more-stringent building codes, higher standards for neighborhood development, and improved inspections, newly developed housing units will likely remain affordable—through lower life-cycle maintenance and repair costs—and desirable over the long term.

These strategies, along with others discussed in the affordable-housing literature, informed RAND's work in the development of policy options for rebuilding affordable housing along Mississippi's Gulf Coast.

Lessons Learned and Best Practices from Previous Natural Disasters

Several common themes emerge in studies about on the short- and long-term effects of natural disasters on the supply of affordable housing:

- Recovery in the housing market often takes longer in low-income neighborhoods and for multifamily rental units than for middle- and upper-income neighborhoods and single-family homes. This was observed, for example, following the Loma Prieta and Northridge earthquakes in California as well as Hurricane Andrew in Florida (Comerio, 1998).
- A marked decline in the supply of low-income housing often follows a disaster. This occurs because, during the rebuilding process, private markets do not find it profitable to replace multifamily, affordable rental housing. This happened, for instance, after Hurricane Andrew in Florida in the early 1990s (Comerio, 1998).
- The disbursement of federal recovery funds may not adequately address the more difficult financial challenges faced by lower-income households in the rebuilding process. After the 1994 Northridge earthquake, for example, regions composed of wealthier homeowners with higher damage costs received more federal assistance than did poorer areas that suffered lower monetary damages but also had fewer alternate sources of financial support (Loukaitou-Sideris and Kamel, 2004).

Combining elements from the literatures on affordable housing and the recoveries from previous natural disasters, RAND researchers distilled four key lessons that may prove valuable in helping to shape Mississippi's efforts to rebuild a sufficient quantity of safe and affordable housing to meet the needs of the displaced population:

- Decisionmakers require timely and accurate data and information about the scale and scope of the damages and about the demographics of the displaced population in order to make effective planning and development decisions.
- In the distribution of federal recovery funds, special priority should be devoted to the needs of lower-income households with limited access to alternate financial resources at their disposal.
- Private-sector capital may play an extremely important role in helping to redevelop the stock of high-quality affordable housing, particularly given current budget challenges at the state and federal level. To maximize the benefits of private investment, public and private sector funds can be coordinated through innovative public-private partnerships, nonprofit arrangements, and market-based incentives.
- To mitigate damages in the event of future natural disasters, new affordable-housing units should incorporate stringent minimum building-safety codes (such as higher wind-resistance ratings in coastal areas subject to hurricanes or higher foundations in areas prone to flooding or storm surge).

Preliminary Assessment of the Extent and Scope of Damage Sustained by Affordable Housing in Coastal Mississippi

To improve our understanding of the scale and nature of the affordable-housing problem currently facing Mississippi, several key data sources were analyzed to develop a preliminary estimate of the hurricane damages. Our preliminary analysis indicated that the hurricane hit hardest in the more developed areas of the three coastal counties of Mississippi—Hancock, Harrison, and Jackson. This area has many households with incomes below the federal poverty level (FPL), and many more with below-average income. Across the three counties, households with income below the U.S. median level occupied two-thirds of the housing units; in Hancock and Harrison counties, the figure was closer to three-quarters.

For the three coastal counties, RAND estimated that about 81,000 units—representing more than half of the total housing stock—were exposed to potential damage from the storm surge or flooding, and that about one-third of these units were occupied by households living below the U.S. median income level. This suggests that at least 27,000 affordable housing units may need to be rebuilt within the three coastal counties alone. These estimates, however, are likely to understate the actual size of the problem. First, the estimates are based on 2000 census data and thus do not account for new housing units that have been built in the intervening years. Second, the estimates do not account for potential damage in nonflooding zones due to high winds. As such, the actual number of affordable housing units that may need to be rebuilt within the three counties could be much higher.

In some areas, the percentage of units devastated by the storm was much higher. In a sample of 6,404 housing units on the Biloxi peninsula, for example, over 80 percent experienced extensive or catastrophic damage, and most of these were occupied by families living below the U.S. median income level. Households with incomes below 150 percent of the FPL occupied 40 percent of the housing units in this sample area.

Such findings present a compelling motivation for the state of Mississippi to devote explicit consideration to the needs of the lower-income population during the planning and rebuilding efforts, working to ensure that the region includes an adequate supply of affordable housing. The task of rebuilding affordable housing, however, involves an array of daunting challenges. This report presents a suite of policy options that may help Mississippi to overcome these challenges.

Policy Options

In this paper, we present more than 25 policy options to support the development of affordable housing in Mississippi. In keeping with the goals of the Governor's Commission, many of these options are designed to be implemented by government bodies at the state and local levels. Some of the options, however, will require partnerships with federal agencies, with non-profit organizations, or with private-sector participants. For clarity, the options can be organized into five categories that address different specific needs:

- *Improving Oversight and Coordination:* The options in this category are designed to ensure that the necessary institutional capacity is in place to oversee the affordable-housing redevelopment efforts, and that thorough, objective analysis is available to inform long-term policy decisions. In particular, this category includes several specific analysis tasks as well as the formation of a new institution to coordinate the rebuilding efforts.
- *Increasing the Quantity of Affordable Housing Units:* This category comprises options to promote the development of a sufficient quantity of affordable-housing units to support the area's residents and employment base. The options include additional potential sources of subsidies for affordable housing, regulatory or incentive-based programs to encourage developers to increase the supply of affordable housing, innovative financing options to reduce the cost of affordable housing, and strategies to ensure that the stock of affordable housing does not decline over the long term.
- *Increasing the Quality and Safety of Affordable Housing:* These options are designed to ensure that affordable housing conforms to stringent minimum health and safety codes. In order to keep costs low, developers may feel pressed to compromise on the construction quality of affordable housing. Designed to prevent this problem, the options in this category will help to improve residents' quality of life in the short run and to mitigate damage in the event of future disasters.
- *Increasing Long-Term Affordability Through Lower Life-Cycle Costs:* This category includes options for increasing the long-term affordability of housing through lower maintenance and utility costs. While mortgage and rental payments are important, the amount of money that households must spend on monthly utility bills and periodic repairs represents another important ingredient the affordability of housing. Accordingly, the options presented in this category create opportunities and incentives for builders, lenders, and insurers to include consideration of the long-run operational costs of a home during the development and marketing of their products.

- *Promoting Local Involvement:* The options provided within this category are designed to promote greater local involvement in planning decisions as well as in the rebuilding efforts. Lower-income residents and affordable-housing advocates have the largest stake in the outcome of Mississippi's efforts to redevelop the stock of affordable housing, and thus they should be well represented within the planning process. At the same time, Mississippi communities will certainly benefit if local contractors and the local workforce can plan a larger role in the rebuilding efforts. The options in this category reflect these considerations.

Of the many options presented in the paper, several appear to be especially important in supporting Mississippi's efforts to rebuild a sufficient quantity of safe, affordable housing to meet the needs of the displaced population. Three of these require action as quickly as possible in order to provide the maximum level of benefits. First, there is a clear need to develop more accurate information to support planners and policymakers in the Gulf region, as decisions are currently being made without sufficient data on how much housing is needed, where it is needed, and what types of zoning and building standards should be employed to minimize losses in the event of future disasters. In particular, policy researchers should address three critical questions in the near term:

- What are the long-term housing needs for different regions and population groups?
- What are barriers that Mississippi will face in ensuring an adequate supply of affordable housing, and how can these be overcome?
- What are some of the best practices from around the country that can be applied in Mississippi?

Second, to ensure that the process of redeveloping affordable housing in Mississippi is managed as effectively and efficiently as possible, the state might consider forming a new institutional entity to oversee the housing recovery efforts. Among other roles, this entity would coordinate and prioritize funding allocations, provide outreach and education to residents and local communities, and coordinate with other regional planning efforts. Third, to mitigate damages in the event of future natural disasters, state and local jurisdictions could institute minimum building-safety codes and enhance the institutional capacity for permitting and inspecting new construction before the rebuilding efforts begin in earnest.

Two additional options also appear to hold much promise, though the time line for these is less urgent. First, state and local governments can set regional goals for affordable housing to ensure that a significant portion of workers can live in the communities in which they are employed. Strategies to achieve these goals include developing affordable-housing trust funds, working with lenders to develop lower-rate mortgages for affordable housing, encouraging employers to offer affordable-housing assistance, providing incentives to stimulate public-private affordable-housing partnerships, and restructuring zoning and building codes to allow for efficient, safe, and lower-cost modular-home construction. Second, policymakers can create incentives for builders to construct homes that use less water and energy and that are easier to maintain in order to facilitate longer-term housing affordability.

Acknowledgments

We would like to express our thanks to the numerous volunteers involved with the Governor's Commission with whom we had the opportunity to work. Their dedication was inspiring, and we are grateful for the welcome we received from everyone we met in Mississippi. We also appreciate the manner in which the input we offered to the Commission was handled and incorporated by Henry Barbour, Trent Walker, and Brian Sanderson. Thanks are also due to Gavin Smith, who provided us with insights on housing issues and directed us to some of the key literature in this area. We would also like to acknowledge Todd Davison of the Federal Emergency Management Agency (FEMA), who provided access to extremely useful data. In addition, we offer thanks to our reviewers Rae Archibald and Neil Richman for their constructive ideas that significantly strengthened this report. Finally, we appreciate the investment made by RAND in this effort and the support of Jack Riley and Debra Knopman who provided us with the opportunity to pursue this work.

Abbreviations

ABFE	advisory base flood elevation
CDE	community development entity
CEO	chief executive officer
CLT	community land trust
DHHS	U.S. Department of Health and Human Services
DOE	U.S. Department of Energy
EAH	employer-assisted housing
EEED	Environment, Energy, and Economic Development Program
EPA	U.S. Environmental Protection Agency
FEMA	Federal Emergency Management Agency
FIRM	flood insurance rate map
FMR	fair-market rent
FPL	federal poverty level
GIS	geographic information system
HUD	U.S. Department of Housing and Urban Development
HWM	high water mark
IFG	Individual and Family Grants
ISE	Infrastructure, Safety, and Environment
LEED	Leadership in Energy and Environmental Design
LIDAR	light detection and ranging
LIHEAP	Low Income Household Energy Assistance Program
MDA	Mississippi Development Authority

MHC	Mississippi Housing Corporation
NGO	nongovernmental organization
NIMBY	not in my back yard
NLIHC	National Low Income Housing Coalition
NOAA	National Oceanic and Atmospheric Administration
NVOAD	National Voluntary Organizations Active in Disaster
PFI	private finance initiatives
PPP	public-private partnership
RGSPI	RAND Gulf States Policy Institute
RSDE	residential substantial damage estimate
SBA	Small Business Administration
SIL	surge inundation limit
UMCOR	United Methodist Committee on Relief

CHAPTER ONE

Introduction

Hurricane Katrina and Its Aftermath

Hurricane Katrina, one of the largest and most violent storms ever recorded in the United States, left a blanket of destruction along the Gulf Coast from the Alabama border west to Texas that covered about 90,000 square miles. Mississippi took the brunt of the winds and a storm surge that rose to more than 30 feet, erasing in a matter of hours not only lives but also homes and assets that will take years to replace.

The sheer scale of what happened to Mississippi in the last days of August 2005 is unparalleled in our nation's history. More than 134,000 homes were damaged and at least 65,000 were completely destroyed. In the aftermath of Hurricane Katrina, more than a million households have received federal assistance thus far, and countless agencies, organizations, and volunteers have responded to assist affected communities and individuals. More than 50,000 Mississippians from more than 18,000 households are living in trailers, while others live in hotel rooms in one of the 44 states and the District of Columbia that have received evacuees from the Gulf region.

Across Mississippi, the Federal Emergency Management Agency (FEMA) offered assistance to 47 affected counties, but the coastal areas sustained the most damage. Of the first 56 documented deaths in Louisiana, Mississippi, and Alabama, 50 of them occurred in Harrison County, one of the six southern counties that sustained the most damage in Mississippi. Notably, most of the state's development is concentrated in the three counties that lie along the coast—Hancock, Harrison, and Jackson—and these counties received the most damage from Katrina.

As in New Orleans, recovering from Hurricane Katrina is made more challenging because some of the hardest-hit communities are also some of the poorest and most densely populated. In 2004, residents of Mississippi had the lowest per-capita personal income in the United States—$24,379—more than 25 percent less than the national average. In addition, Mississippi's housing stock is relatively old, and state and local officials with whom we spoke have indicated that building codes are neither strict nor consistently enforced across the state. Collectively, these issues suggest that the hardest-hit communities will have significant challenges in rebuilding. On the one hand, low-income residents have limited means to invest in the rebuilding effort. On the other hand, lessors have less incentive to rebuild affordable housing in poorer communities than to invest in more affluent areas.

Governor's Commission for Recovery, Reconstruction, Renewal

Within a week after the passage of Hurricane Katrina, Mississippi Governor Haley Barbour began to develop an organizational framework to plan and support rebuilding efforts in the most heavily damaged areas of Mississippi. These early efforts led to the creation of the Governor's Commission for Recovery, Reconstruction, Renewal. Chaired by James Barksdale, founder and former chief executive officer (CEO) of Netscape Communications Corporation, and funded by private donations, the Commission received a mandate from Governor Barbour to explore a wide range of options for rebuilding the damaged areas, focusing on strategies to restore what was lost over the short term and to create even stronger and more integrated communities moving forward.

The Commission's basic mission was to (1) solicit the best ideas for recovery, reconstruction, and renewal from both public and private sectors, (2) develop a broad vision for a better Gulf Coast and southern Mississippi, and (3) involve local citizens and elected officials in the process of developing and endorsing these ideas. Under the Governor's directive, the role of the Commission was to be advisory in nature with a great deal of focus on supporting local leaders through an inclusive and participatory process. Specifically, the Commission was asked to provide local leaders with ideas and information to help them envision what their region could look like five, ten, twenty, or thirty years from now and to recommend strategies and tools for achieving these goals. Final implementation decisions would then be left almost exclusively to local officials with support from the private and nonprofit sectors.

Two types of committees carried out the Commission's work. First, *county and regional committees* were charged with conducting open, town hall–type meetings and public forums to provide local citizens with the opportunity to voice their views. Between September and December of 2005, the effective term of the Commission, town-hall meetings were convened in 33 counties, and over 50 public forums were held. Second, *issue committees* were formed to evaluate challenges and identify opportunities within specific sectors—e.g., infrastructure, finance, agriculture and forestry, tourism, defense and government contracting, small business and entrepreneurship, education, health and human services, and nongovernmental organizations (NGOs)—during the renewal process.

At the outset, the Commission examined the work of groups appointed after other national disasters such as the 1900 Galveston Hurricane, the Mississippi Flood of 1927, and Hurricane Camille in Mississippi in 1969. Camille, a category-five storm, left 130 dead, destroyed 3,800 homes in six southern counties, and wrought damages on the order of $9 billion in inflation-adjusted dollars. Katrina, in contrast, was categorized as a strong category-three storm when it hit the Mississippi coast, but it was far larger than Camille and had a higher storm surge. As a result, Katrina left more than 230 dead and completely destroyed 65,000 homes in Mississippi alone, and the estimated recovery bill within the three most affected states—Mississippi, Louisiana, and Alabama—amounts to nearly $100 billion.

One of the early conclusions from the analysis of previous post-disaster recovery efforts was that the process of identifying problems and suggesting solutions, while important, is not sufficient to achieve long-term reforms. Along with basic tactical strategies, important implementation and accountability issues also must be addressed. Because Mississippi failed to engage these important institutional issues fully after 1969—for example, by not mandating minimum building-safety codes in hurricane-prone areas—the state now faces much larger recovery, rebuilding, and renewal challenges following Hurricane Katrina. With this consideration in mind, the Commission placed a great deal of focus on implementation and accountability. The Commission was also guided by the belief that local governments and citizens should have the opportunity to explore a range of options for rebuilding their communities and should accept responsibility for key decisions, and that they would benefit from developing alliances with nonprofit, private, state, and federal institutions.

In addition to the activities of individual committees, the Commission also staged a six-day "Mississippi Renewal Forum." About 200 professionals in all—including about 100 from Mississippi and a comparable number from other areas in the United States—gathered to discuss and develop plans for rebuilding the 11 coastal cities and the 120 miles of coastal region where the damage was worst. The professionals offered expertise in numerous fields, including architecture, regional and community planning, civil and transportation engineering, environmentalism, law, retailing, economics, sociology, public policy, and communications. They worked to develop plans for more sustainable living patterns at all income levels, suggesting strategies to rebuild communities with pedestrian-friendly streets, more attractive transit options, and a better mix of commercial, office, and residential uses.

Combined, the renewal forum and the activities of the individual Commission committees yielded some 240 separate recommendations, the products of four months of intensive research and public discussions and 50,000 hours of contribution by 500 volunteers. At the end of December 2005, the Commission prepared a final report, entitled "After Katrina—Building Back Better Than Ever," summarizing these recommendations. The report was delivered to the Governor on December 31 and released to the public in mid-January. The recommendations fell into four broad categories:

- Infrastructure, including land use, transportation, public services, and housing
- Economic development, including tourism, small businesses, agriculture, forestry, marine resources, and defense and government contracting
- Human services, including education, health and human services, and NGOs
- Other special considerations, including finance, long-term policy recommendations, and a roadmap to greater accountability.

Early in 2006, the task of implementing many of the Commission's recommendations was assigned to a new entity based out of the Governor's Office with staff located in several of the coastal counties. This group will coordinate government assistance at all levels and assemble a package of advisory help for local jurisdictions. Adhering to Mississippi's tradition of local accountability, it will be left to county and municipal jurisdictions to pass and enforce ordinances implementing the policy recommendations perceived as offering the greatest benefit to their citizens.

RAND's Role

In the first month of its establishment, the Commission quickly realized that providing adequate housing for its citizens would be not only one of the most urgent rebuilding tasks, but also one of the most complex and difficult goals to achieve. Moreover, it became clear that the housing issue would have important ramifications across all sectors. Recognizing that some of the hardest-hit communities were also some of the poorest, that these communities provided an essential component of the workforce for major businesses along the Mississippi Gulf Coast, and that the most immediate needs within these communities were related to housing, the Commission determined that the task of providing "affordable" housing would be an essential element in rebuilding the economy. The Commission judged the issue of affordable housing to be of even greater importance in light of the experience from prior disasters within the United States, which shows that recovering a sufficient supply of high-quality, affordable housing is at best an arduous undertaking, and that, in most cases, the supply of affordable housing suffers a permanent decline.

In November and December 2005, RAND Corporation researchers traveled to Mississippi and offered to work with the Commission and provide assistance to the Affordable Housing Subcommittee of the Infrastructure Issues Committee. During this period, RAND researchers collaborated with the Housing Subcommittee members and the Commission staff, providing real-time assistance and support and furnishing information and inputs to the process of developing recommendations. The researchers provided support in identifying and developing a wide range of recommendations and options that could help local communities in dealing with the housing issue. The researchers also assisted in the preparation of the affordable-housing section of the Commission's final report.

In addition to working with the Housing subcommittee members, RAND researchers spoke with members of other Governor's Commission committees, such as Infrastructure and Finance, to facilitate a coordinated approach to housing issues. RAND researchers also interacted with other external public agencies as well as nonprofit and private entities concerned with the redevelopment of affordable housing in Mississippi. These included FEMA, the U.S. Department of Housing and Urban Development (HUD), the Mississippi Housing Corporation (MHC), the Mississippi Development Authority (MDA), local governments in cities such as Biloxi and Ocean Springs, major businesses and employers such as the Isle of Capri Casino, and grant-making institutions.

At the outset of RAND's involvement, it became clear that the availability of data on the scope and nature of affordable-housing needs in Mississippi following the hurricane was extremely limited, and that such data would necessarily provide an important basis for developing all subsequent recommendations. RAND researchers therefore assisted in analyzing some of the preliminary data on housing needs. Most notably, geographic information system (GIS) analytic methods were used to perform a preliminary assessment of the demographics of the affected population and the status of housing before and after the hurricane. This preliminary assessment helped to ensure that the affordable-housing options that RAND described would be relevant to the population's needs.

RAND's Approach

This report, which follows the release of the final report by the Commission, presents RAND's work in support of the Commission's efforts to address affordable-housing issues in Mississippi. It also provides supplementary information gathered and assessed subsequent to the release of the Commission report.

When RAND engaged in the task of providing the Commission with assistance on the issue of affordable housing, it began by considering the following questions:

1. How is "affordable housing" defined and what are some of general affordable-housing issues faced by different regions in the United States? What are the critical challenges in providing affordable housing and what strategies are available to deal with these challenges?

2. How have affordable-housing issues been addressed in the wake of other natural disasters in the United States? What lessons have we learned and what best practices can we take away from previous natural-disaster experiences?

3. What are the extent and scope of damage sustained by Mississippi relative to affordable housing? What types of affordable-housing needs might the state of Mississippi consider addressing during the rebuilding process, and at what scale?

4. What range of policy options would prove most useful as Mississippi strives to address its current affordable-housing issues? What options would enable the state to (a) make long-term, effective affordable-housing policy decisions; (b) provide an adequate supply of affordable housing and increase its affordability to the general population; (c) build higher-quality, safer affordable housing that can better withstand future disasters; (d) ensure long-term affordability, taking into consideration life-cycle costs related to durability and energy and water consumption; and (e) encourage greater local participation in the process of rebuilding?

To gain perspective on these important questions, we conducted interviews and collected on-site data in conjunction with the Commission's activities. In addition, we reviewed the literature on general issues concerning the supply and quality of affordable housing and on specific challenges related to the recovery of affordable housing following previous disasters in the United States. We also reviewed best practices and precedents for restructuring zoning and building codes and for pursuing long-term affordability and sustainability in the wake of natural disasters such as Hurricane Andrew in Florida, Hurricane Hugo in Georgia and the Carolinas, and the Loma Prieta and Northridge earthquakes in California.

Drawing upon observations within the literature as well as our own research efforts, this paper presents a range of promising policy and implementation options that state and federal governments, local communities, NGOs, and private companies could employ to help ensure an adequate supply of safe, high-quality, affordable housing in coastal Mississippi.

Report Outline

This report is organized into five chapters. In this introduction, Chapter One, we have described the background and context for this work. Chapter Two presents the definition of affordable housing used in the report, reviews the extent of the housing shortage, discusses barriers to ensuring an adequate housing supply, and introduces general strategies to reduce the shortage. Chapter Three provides a comparative assessment of the housing in coastal Mississippi before and after Katrina to provide a better understanding of the scope and nature of affordable housing needs within the state. It also provides a literature review of lessons learned from other disasters, which are used as the basis for formulating options to address current affordable-housing challenges in the Mississippi Gulf Coast. Chapter Four discusses a set of options for managing and coordinating the efforts to rebuild affordable housing in Mississippi, for enhancing the supply of affordable housing, for improving the quality and safety of affordable housing, for promoting long-term affordability through lower housing life-cycle costs, and for encouraging greater local participation in the planning and rebuilding efforts. Chapter Five offers conclusions and provides a summary of the options, discussing the appropriate time frame for implementation, the relative costs, the specific issues addressed (quantity, quality, long-term affordability, or coordination), and the nature of institutional involvement. Finally, the appendix presents a more detailed description of the data and methods used in the GIS analysis.

CHAPTER TWO

Affordable Housing and Lessons Learned from Other Natural Disasters

What Is Affordable Housing?

Affordable housing can be defined in myriad ways, both quantitatively and qualitatively. The most commonly accepted quantitative definition specifies that housing can be considered affordable if a household is not required to spend more than 30 percent of its income on mortgage or rent payments (Feldman, 2002), although the exact income-percentage cutoff may vary slightly in different states (in Arizona, for example, the designated cutoff is 28 percent; AHC, 2002). In addition, some formal definitions of affordable housing include not only cost, but also specify that the housing should be "physically adequate" and not overcrowded (Field, 1997; AHC, 2002).

Many authors use the phrase *affordable housing* to refer specifically to government-sponsored or otherwise subsidized housing. For example, Charles Field (1997, p. 802) defined affordable housing as "physically adequate housing that is made available . . . by government or special arrangement . . . to [those who] . . . could not [otherwise] afford the . . . housing."

In this report, we adopt a rather broad definition for affordable housing, one that includes any housing options that meet minimum building codes and require not more than 30 percent of a household's income for rental or mortgage payments. The housing may be subsidized or not, and it may include owner-occupied or rental units.

Within this broad framework, the goal of finding adequate, affordable housing can be viewed as a problem for both lower-income and middle-income groups. Families within these income distributions often struggle to find affordable housing for two common reasons. In some cases, lower-income households live in homes or apartments that are beyond their means. This reduces the supply of housing for the next-higher income group, forcing them to pay more for housing than they should as well. This snowball effect can extend through the housing stock up to moderate-income households (AHC, 2002).

In other cases, most commonly in suburban locations, typical zoning practices can limit the variety of housing options provided. This forces local retail employees, blue-collar workers, and others who earn low to moderate wages either to commute long distances or to pay more for housing than they can afford (Field, 1997). For this reason, we add a caveat to the definition of affordable housing. Specifically, we posit that a key goal for communities on the Gulf Coast should be to not only provide enough affordable housing in aggregate, but also ensure that the spatial distribution of affordable units aligns with locations of suitable employment opportunities. This will allow communities in coastal Mississippi to avoid the problems of resort-based communities such as Aspen, Colorado, where people cannot afford to live near where they work. By committing to the goal of developing sufficient housing options near employment opportunities, communities will help to reduce the stress on working-family incomes, reduce the potential for lengthy commutes, reduce traffic congestion on the road network, and perhaps reduce pollution problems as well.

Understanding the Affordability Gap

Assessing the shortage of affordable housing is a critical input to the planning process for housing reconstruction on the Gulf Coast. The "affordability gap" concept provides a useful lens through which to view this issue. At the household level, the affordability gap refers to the difference between 30 percent of a family's income and the cost of available housing in good condition within the area (Downs, 2003). At the regional level, the gap corresponds to the difference between the number of households within each income range and the number of affordable housing units available to those households. According to some definitions, the gap encompasses not only households needing to spend more than 30 percent of their income on housing, but also households forced to live in substandard or overcrowded housing (AHC, 2002).

There have been some attempts to estimate the affordability gap at national and regional scales, and these are reviewed below. However, while quantifying the affordability gap provides an important framework for understanding the need for housing (and is doubly critical for rebuilding after a natural disaster), the scale at which relevant data are tracked is often inadequate to the task of calculating good estimates at the local level (DiPasquale, 1999). For example, housing quantity and price data aggregated at the county level, or even at the municipal level (depending on the size of the city), may not be sufficient for understanding the ability of lower-income households to find affordable housing within a reasonable distance from employment opportunities. Unfortunately, data on the quality of housing are even more limited than data on quantity and price, making it even more difficult to provide accurate estimates of the quality gap in housing.

With these caveats in mind, it is useful now to review the results of prior studies on the affordability gap. In the 2003 *American Housing Survey*, researchers estimated that 7.5 million households across the country were severely burdened by their housing costs, spending more than half their income on rent or mortgage payments (U.S. Department of Commerce, 2003). Results from the survey also suggested that the United States was 1.6 million units short of affordable housing.

Some regions have attempted to characterize the gap at specific income levels. For example, a study of the Minneapolis metropolitan area found that more than three-quarters of households earning less than a third of the local median income lived in housing that was not affordable (Feldman, 2002). This is similar to results from Arizona, where researchers identified significant affordability gaps for households earning less than 50 percent of the median income within the state. While the gaps narrowed for families with higher income levels, even households earning the median income level within the state faced some gaps (AHC, 2002).

While we did not find an affordability-gap analysis focused specifically on Mississippi, there are other sources of data that provide insight to the state's affordable-housing problems. For example, the National Low Income Housing Coalition (NLIHC, 2005) presents data on rental units and renter income levels drawn from a variety of sources. For 2005, it estimated that the fair-market rent[1] (FMR) for a one-bedroom apartment in Mississippi was around $450 per month. For a household to be able to "afford" such an apartment (in other words, to spend less than 30 percent of its income on the rent), the members of the household would need to earn at least half of the state's median income. Following similar logic, the members of the household would need to earn very close to the state's median income to afford the FMR for a two-bedroom apartment. By this criterion, less than 50 percent of the renting households within Mississippi could afford a two-bedroom apartment, let alone a three- or four-bedroom apartment. The study also provided similar statistics for the three coastal counties in Mississippi. Here, the average rents were slightly higher, but so too were the average wages, so the affordability calculations came out roughly the same.

Researchers point to several reasons why the housing affordability gap persists despite the variety of programs and subsidies put in place by federal and state governments. First, most of the government housing policies are aimed at home ownership, whereas many of the households most in need are renters who could not afford to buy a home even with substantial assistance (Downs, 2003). Second, many of the projects developed through the low-income housing tax credits still need additional subsidies to make them affordable to the lowest-income populations (Belsky, 2001). Finally, even if the cost of housing were to decrease substantially, a large percentage of the people for whom housing is currently unaffordable would still find housing to be unaffordable; the existing gap between incomes and housing costs is that large (Feldman, 2002).

Challenges to Improving the Supply of Affordable Housing

Plans to rebuild the Gulf Coast will need to take into account the variety of barriers that continue to hinder attempts to improve the supply of quality affordable housing.

Rising cost of land and housing prices. With the anticipated level of investment along the Gulf Coast following Hurricane Katrina, rising land costs could become an increasingly important issue. If the land is expensive, after all, then it will be difficult to build affordable housing for those on the lower end of the income scale. This should be taken as a cautionary note for devastated communities planning to embrace smart growth and new-urbanist principles in their redevelopment strategies.[2] There are, to be sure, many potential benefits to these planning concepts, including reduced sprawl, reduced reliance on the automobile, more vibrant communities, and enhanced "livability." At the same time, however, many of the communities that have used these approaches in the past have witnessed upward pressure on hous-

---

[1] The FMR for an area is the amount that would be needed to pay the gross rent (shelter rent plus utilities) of privately owned, decent, and safe rental housing of a modest (nonluxury) nature with standard amenities.

[2] Smart growth plans are efforts to reduce the impacts of urban sprawl. Developed and promulgated by the "new urbanist" movement, smart growth strategies typically promote features such as dense, mixed-use zoning patterns and "walkable" community designs.

ing prices, resulting in a displacement of lower-income households (Downs, 2003). The same phenomenon could easily occur in communities along the Gulf Coast that choose to embrace smart growth principles unless proactive steps are taken to protect the supply of affordable housing.

Lack of knowledge about housing options. Lack of knowledge about affordable-housing options and related financial issues on the part of lower-income households has also been noted as a barrier to affordable housing (AHC, 2002). Many people are not familiar with the various programs that may be available to them, nor do they possess a sophisticated understanding of household finance and money-management strategies.

Zoning issues. Another critical barrier relates to zoning issues. The basic problem is that many communities have adopted specific zoning regulations—e.g., minimum lot sizes, minimum building setbacks, stringent design guidelines, or limitations on the types of buildings that can be constructed—that effectively prevent the development of less-expensive multifamily-housing options such as apartments or condominiums. In certain cases, the preclusion of affordable multifamily housing through zoning regulations may have been unintentional; in others, however, the outcome appears to have been deliberate, driven by a "not in my back yard" (NIMBY) attitude on the part of more affluent communities opposed to the creation of affordable housing within their midst (HUD, 1991; AHC, 2002).

Additional factors. Other barriers to affordable housing include developer fees and minimum parking requirements (which drive up the cost of new homes), a lack of suitable employment opportunities, and a gap between prevailing wages and the cost of living. Indeed, some have concluded that the affordable-housing problem should really be viewed as more of an income problem than a supply or cost problem since the prospects for reducing the cost of housing are limited by physical construction costs and the market for land (Feldman, 2002). Finally, the challenges and solutions for affordable housing differ by region, and many of the national policies are simply not flexible enough to handle significant regional differences, despite the fact that the states themselves administer many of them (Neiman and Bush, 2004).

Strategies to Address the Affordability Gap

The debate about affordable housing often boils down to disagreements over how to reduce the affordability gap, and many of the arguments focus on whether it is more appropriate to reduce the cost of housing or to increase the ability of people to pay for housing. Some who view low incomes as the source of the problem suggest that supplementing income may be the more effective route (for example, by increasing food stamps or other income-improving measures). Others maintain that increasing wages is the more difficult task and that it may be simpler to lower the cost of housing through strategies such as lower interest rates, lower down-payment requirements, or other options. There are also disagreements on the roles for the government, the private sector, and individual households. Within this report, we do not explicitly embrace one perspective over another, but rather highlight the options—whatever their source—that would appear to offer the greatest promise in supporting affordable-housing goals as coastal Mississippi rebuilds in the wake of Hurricane Katrina.

Some of the most commonly suggested strategies for addressing affordable housing issues include the following:

- *Improving education.* Educating people on financial and housing options can improve their ability to find and secure high-quality, affordable housing.
- *Lowering housing costs.* Lowering the costs by reducing fees, changing codes and zoning ordinances to allow for new technologies and housing styles to be introduced, reducing mortgage and insurance costs, providing additional finance options, and fostering public-private partnerships are strategies that provide more opportunities for families to find affordable housing.
- *Increasing the quality of affordable-housing supply.* Much of the affordable-housing stock is in disrepair and expensive to maintain. By applying more-stringent building codes, higher standards for neighborhood development, and improved inspections, newly developed housing units will likely remain affordable—through lower life-cycle maintenance and repair costs—and desirable over the long term.

Finally, some researchers have suggested that the prevalence of policies focusing on home ownership rather than rental opportunities has exacerbated the affordability gap. On the other hand, home ownership among the lower-income population can be an important driver for community development and foster increased civic involvement by residents. Studies have shown, for instance, that educational outcomes improve for children in communities with significant home ownership levels, and that home equity can represent a significant portion of household wealth for families from lower-income groups (Phillips, 2005).

Lessons About Affordable Housing from Other Natural Disasters

Affordable-Housing Issues

Even before the arrival of Hurricane Katrina, Mississippi faced challenging affordable-housing issues. With the extreme devastation wrought in coastal communities by high winds, flooding, and the storm surge, these problems have grown even more formidable. In considering potential options to promote the development of enough affordable housing to meet the needs of the displaced population following such a catastrophic event, it is therefore useful to review lessons from past national disasters within the United States.

Recent studies have examined the impact of natural disasters on affordable housing, both within the United States and abroad. Many of these studies have focused on disasters in high-density areas such as San Francisco, Los Angeles, and coastal Florida, and it is therefore necessary to exercise caution in extrapolating their results to the less densely populated Mississippi coast. Even so, the prior literature suggests three important themes that may be highly relevant for the post-Katrina affordable-housing market:

- The housing market generally takes longer to recover in low-income neighborhoods.
- The quantity of low-income housing units often suffers a long-term decline.
- The distribution of disaster relief funds is typically based on the magnitude of the financial loss suffered by a household rather than the level of financial resources available to the

household; as a result, wealthier residents (with homes that are more expensive to repair or replace) tend to receive a larger share of the available funds despite the fact that poorer residents face greater financial challenges in securing the necessary resources to rebuild.

In a study by Comerio (1998) of the recovery efforts following four previous natural disasters in the United States—including Hurricane Hugo in the Carolinas and Georgia, Hurricane Andrew in Florida, and the Loma Prieta and Northridge earthquakes in California— low-income neighborhoods consistently recovered more slowly than did wealthier areas, a finding that was reinforced in subsequent work by Loukaitou-Sideris and Kamel (2004). For instance, after the two California earthquakes, most homes were repaired or replaced within a year, but this was not generally the case for low-income homes and rental units, and multifamily buildings often fell through the cracks. After Hurricane Andrew, while most of the housing units were rebuilt within two to three years, primarily the middle- and upper-income homes, rather than the low-income units, were built again.

One of the reasons that rebuilding can take longer in low-income neighborhoods is that the homes in such areas are often at greater risk. In fact, several authors have defined the term *disaster* as an environmental hazard impinging on vulnerable populations (Bolin and Stanford, 1998). There are two separate factors at play. First, the homes may be located in less desirable (and hence cheaper) areas that are more susceptible to damage, such as along fault lines or within flood zones. Second, the homes themselves may be in dilapidated condition to begin with, or may be built to older, substandard safety codes (Lindell and Prater, 2003). In the Loma Prieta earthquake, for example, the 1,300 housing units destroyed in Oakland were all located in 10 unreinforced hotels that served as the last line of affordable housing for poor and elderly residents in a city with skyrocketing property values (Comerio, 1998).

Even where low-income households do not face higher vulnerability to natural disasters based on location or structural factors, they may encounter greater financial difficulty during the recovery phase (Chang and Miles, 2003). Low-income households living in single-family dwellings, for example, are less likely to have the financial and institutional resources (such as insurance) to rebuild (Lindell and Prater, 2003). As a result, low-income households displaced by a disaster tend to transition into permanent housing more slowly than do others in the community, and, in some cases, they come to accept as permanent housing that which was at first temporary (Lindell and Prater, 2003). Moreover, because many low-income families rent rather than own, recovery is often out of their hands. Simply stated, there is no guarantee that private markets will replace affordable housing during the rebuilding process. When affordable housing has been damaged in prior disasters, lessors frequently repair and rebuild their rental units to higher code and design standards. This results in higher rents, which often places the units out of financial reach for previous tenants. In turn, the demand for remaining affordable-housing options within the community only intensifies (Petterson, 1999).

Following Hurricane Andrew, most of the middle class returned to the areas most devastated, but a large portion of the lower-income groups did not. In part, this occurred because the employment base did not reach its former level, but it is also clear that the limited redevelopment of affordable rental units served to drive out the poorest part of the populations. After the Northridge earthquake, low-income housing did not return to pre-earthquake levels.

After Hugo, there was a similar decline in low-income rental units because many lessors chose not to repair damaged property. While these outcomes were driven to some extent by market realities, they were also exacerbated by the lack of coordination between the public and private sectors (Comerio, 1998).

Affordable-housing supplies may also suffer in the wake of disasters because the distribution formulas for recovery funds tend to favor wealthier residents who own more expensive homes that cost more to repair or rebuild. In their examination of federal assistance following the Northridge earthquake, for example, Loukaitou-Sideris and Kamel (2004) found that the allocation of funds was based upon the magnitude of the financial losses incurred rather than upon the financial capacity of households to secure funding through alternate channels. As a result, wealthier regions with higher total damage costs and disaster losses received more federal assistance than did poorer areas in which residents suffered lower monetary damages but also had fewer financial resources to pay for housing repair and reconstruction.

Frequently, low-income households, despite tangible economic losses, are simply not eligible for aid from the largest available sources of funding. After reimbursement by private insurance, federal assistance is the most powerful source of funds for rebuilding. But while FEMA and Small Business Administration (SBA) funds are available to support the rebuilding efforts of individual families, the loans from these agencies are generally restricted to individuals with a steady employment history and a good credit record (Loukaitou-Sideris and Kamel 2004). Thus, disadvantaged households are forced to turn to other funding sources that do not provide the same level of resources.

Following the Northridge earthquake, Individual and Family Grants (IFGs) were available to poor households who did not qualify for SBA loans. IFGs were theoretically available at the maximum level of $22,200. In several study sites, however, Bolin and Stanford (1998) found that grants averaged only five percent of that amount. Moreover, the application process for IFGs was itself confusing; applicants first had to apply for SBA funding and be rejected before they could apply for an IFG.

Low-income households are also more likely to live in multifamily dwellings, for which owners receive less federal and state funds for rebuilding (Comerio, 1998; Loukaitou-Sideris and Kamel, 2004). Following the Loma Prieta earthquake, for instance, no federal programs explicitly targeted the redevelopment of multifamily complexes. Moreover, residents of single-occupancy hotels destroyed in the Loma Prieta earthquake were often ineligible for any funding at all, because they did not live continuously in their hotel rooms (Greene, 1993). With both the Loma Prieta and Northridge earthquakes, SBA loans represented the only federal recovery mechanism for funding the rebuilding of multifamily dwellings. Here again, however, these loans did not cover many structures because of the poor credit of potential borrowers or the large loan amounts required to fund reconstruction (Loukaitou-Sideris and Kamel, 2004). As a result, more complicated financial solutions leveraging other affordable-housing programs had to be pieced together after the disaster had already occurred. Such disasters can thus completely overburden a financial support system that, even during normal times, is unable to supply enough low-income housing (Greene, 1993).

The absence or inadequacy of local institutional capacity to support the redevelopment of affordable housing is another common problem. Where local organizations are not available to identify needs and prioritize funding disbursements, affordable housing is not rebuilt as quickly as higher-end housing, or is not rebuilt at all. Even when there are local organizations to guide the distribution of funding into a community, the results may not be systematic and seldom provide long-term solutions. Rather, the process "is essentially a 'non-system' of recovery aid as it lacks, in its totality, any integrated recovery plans or long-term goals" (Bolin and Stanford, 1998).

Finally, researchers have found that, after disasters, policymakers usually lack information and data about the demographics of households displaced and the extent of damage to homes and apartments (Comerio, 1998; Morrow, 1999). Without such data, recovery planners are often forced to rely on approximate information. For example, after the March 1, 1997, tornado that hit Arkadelphia, Arkansas, officials were forced to rely on aerial photographs and residents' memories to estimate structural needs in the hardest-hit part of the community (Schwab, 1998).

Strategies to Address Affordable Housing After a Natural Disaster

In addition to highlighting challenges, the literature reviewed in this chapter also includes suggested strategies for ensuring that affordable housing is adequately rebuilt after a disaster occurs. These strategies are important for policymakers to consider in the wake of Katrina, and they underlie several of the policy options presented later in this paper.

A key strategy for rebuilding affordable housing after a disaster is to reduce the threat of similar catastrophes in the future by (1) designing homes with higher safety standards to resist damage and (2) developing future recovery plans before the next disaster strikes. Morrow (1999), for example, suggests developing vulnerability maps on a community-by-community basis to document the location and demographics of at-risk populations. Education, mitigation, evacuation, and recovery plans can then be keyed to the data within the map. Socially and economically disadvantaged groups should be included in the preplanning phase so that members have the opportunity to contribute to the plans and will be familiar with the governmental agencies most likely to be involved in rebuilding (Nigg, 1995). In addition, communities should evaluate the capacities of local government and nongovernmental agencies to identify their potential roles in future rebuilding efforts (Berke, Kartez, and Wenger, 1993).

It is also important for communities to get involved in the rebuilding process. Past evidence suggests that rebuilding efforts will typically be more successful in areas supported by well-organized community organizations, even if there are insufficient funds for rebuilding. Community groups can more readily communicate needs to outside agencies, and they can also receive and effectively redirect outside sources of funds to projects that need the most help, such as affordable housing (Loukaitou-Sideris, 2004; Comerio, 1998; Berke, Kartez, and Wenger, 1993).

In allocating recovery funds, governments and agencies can provide stronger support for affordable housing by accounting for the demographic and financial diversity among the populations they serve. In the case of the Northridge earthquake, this did not occur. Despite the existence of a predisaster mitigation plan, the flow of funding was mismatched with local circumstances. Even though 80 percent of the damaged housing units were located in multifamily developments, with low-income housing particularly affected, recovery funds were targeted to middle-class owners of single-family housing (Wu and Lindell, 2004). It is perhaps no surprise, then, that the level of affordable housing did not fully recover following the quake.

Another strategy that may prove useful is for the federal government to channel recovery funds through local nonprofit housing corporations (Bolin and Stanford, 1998). This approach can help to ensure that the funds are allocated to the most pressing needs, and that the rebuilding process occurs as efficiently as possible. According to Comerio (1998), one local entity should take the lead in assessing needs across the community and then recommend an optimal combination of loans, grants, temporary assistance, or other measures to improve the supply and quality of affordable housing (Comerio, 1998).

In the face of devastation, the initial impulse of a community is often to restore things to their predisaster state. However, post-disaster reconstruction efforts represent a valuable opportunity to make important strides toward the community's longer-term social objectives (Deyle et al., 2005). Recovery efforts in Boone, North Carolina, provide a good example of this idea. To mitigate future flood damages, Boone developed a plan to acquire 15 homes located within a chronic flood zone. Rather than demolishing the structures, however, which would have lessened the supply of affordable housing, the township instead relocated the homes to new low- and moderate-income developments elsewhere in the community. Several of the structures were also donated to Habitat for Humanity and to an antidomestic-violence organization (Deyle et al., 2005). In light of the chronic shortages of affordable housing, it may also be appropriate to increase the level of funding during times of disaster so that larger, more-comprehensive solutions to long-term problems can be pursued. To be effective, of course, such funding must also be coupled with the political will to provide safe homes close to opportunities for secure livelihoods (Bolin and Stanford, 1998).

Summary

In this chapter, we have provided a review of the literature describing challenges in the affordable housing market, both during normal times and in the wake of natural disasters. Through careful examination of the findings from this literature, it is possible to distill several key lessons that may provide useful guidance in the rebuilding efforts in coastal Mississippi following Hurricane Katrina:

- *Define the challenge broadly.* In many areas, the shortage of affordable housing affects middle-income households as well as low-income households. Effective solutions should therefore address the question of supply at multiple income levels.
- *Reduce the cost of affordable housing.* Various strategies such as reduced fees, denser zoning codes, relaxed parking requirements, and more flexible financing and insurance options can reduce the cost of affordable housing.
- *Support the planning process with accurate information.* To support comprehensive planning efforts and investment decisions, as well as to inform education and outreach efforts for populations at risk, it is necessary to develop credible and consistent information on factors such as the quantity, condition, and geographic distribution of affordable housing

units and the number of households requiring housing assistance. In the wake of natural disasters, when there is pressure to make rapid planning and development decisions, providing timely and accurate information becomes even more important.

- *Factor financial need into the distribution of recovery funds.* Although wealthy residents with more expensive homes may suffer larger financial losses in the event of an earthquake, tornado, or hurricane, lower-income residents whose homes have been damaged or destroyed have far fewer financial resources at their disposal. To provide adequate support to affordable housing residents following a natural disaster, the distribution formula for recovery funds should reflect this consideration.
- *Tap local knowledge to identify needs and channel resources.* Involving local stakeholder groups such as nonprofit housing authorities to identify needs and channel funds can help streamline rebuilding efforts and also ensure that the concerns of lower-income residents are taken into consideration within the planning process.
- *Mitigate future damages through appropriate building standards.* Evidence from prior disasters indicates that older buildings designed with insufficient safety standards routinely suffer the greatest damages. By rebuilding affordable housing units with updated safety codes, the loss of life and level of damage sustained in future disasters can be greatly reduced.

These six lessons underlie many of the policy options presented later in this paper.

CHAPTER THREE

Affordable Housing in Coastal Mississippi Before and After Katrina

In this chapter, we describe data on housing and household characteristics in the three coastal counties of Mississippi—Hancock, Harrison, and Jackson—that sustained the highest levels of damage during Hurricane Katrina. We compiled this information by using GIS technology to analyze readily available demographic and hurricane-related data sets from the U.S. Census Bureau and FEMA, respectively. Technical details on data sources and analysis methodologies are included in the appendix.

To create descriptive "snapshots" of the area before and after Katrina, we analyzed several key variables and used them to calculate various estimates. First, we determined the total number of households within the three coastal counties according to the last complete census (2000) and categorized them according to relevant characteristics such as median income and age of the housing stock. Next, we estimated the percentage of households located within flood-hazard areas (specifically, areas previously identified as falling within a 100-year flood zone according to FEMA's flood insurance rate map, or FIRM) and the percentage of households within areas believed to have been affected by Katrina's coastal surge (defined by FEMA as the surge inundation limit, or SIL). This should be viewed as a preliminary analysis based on initially available data, and it is not intended to represent a complete picture of pre- or post-Katrina housing issues. Rather, it demonstrates the type of analysis that should be conducted, when updated flood-zone, surge, and damage maps are made available by FEMA, to support policy decisions. The need for further analysis along these lines is addressed within the first set of options that we present later in this paper.

Overview of Indicators, Data, Measures, and Models

Our initial categorization of households focused on data relevant to the risk of structural damage as well as the financial means and potential motivation of residents to rebuild. The selected indicators address the following issues:

- The potential scope of the damages, as indicated by the total number of households within the coastal counties as well as the age of the housing stock (older houses may have been built to less-stringent safety standards, and thus would be more likely to suffer damage from flooding or high winds)
- The financial means of affected households, as indicated by median household income
- The potential motivation of householders to share in the burden of rebuilding areas affected by Katrina, as indicated by whether damaged homes were owner-occupied or not (owner-occupiers may have greater motivation to rebuild their houses, whereas absentee lessors may choose to invest elsewhere, and tenants are free to move on to other rental opportunities).

In short, then, we focused on four specific measures to describe the pre-Katrina conditions of households and their housing.

- *Number of households and population density*
- *Median household income*
- *Housing tenure*, with categories of owner-occupied, rented, or vacant
- *Housing vintage*, with categories being separated at construction either before or after 1980.[1]

We also estimated the counts of households located within potentially flooded and surge-affected areas using GIS analytic methods. In this phase of the analysis, however, it is important to note that our method may have underestimated the number of households actually affected by Hurricane Katrina for three reasons: (1) 2000 census data do not reflect more recent population growth; (2) households are not uniformly distributed across census-block groups (but instead cluster nearer the coast); and (3) we did not consider damages resulting from high winds.

Pre-Katrina Household and Housing Characteristics

Most of Mississippi's recent residential and commercial development has been concentrated in the coastal areas where Hurricane Katrina's storm surge and flooding occurred. As shown in Figure 3.1, population (and housing unit) density was greatest in the coastal cities, particularly in parts of Long Beach, Gulfport, and Biloxi in Harrison County; and in Pascagoula and Moss Point in Jackson County.

Across the three coastal counties of Mississippi, households with incomes below the U.S. median level occupied two-thirds of the housing units, and 12 percent lived below 150 percent of the federal poverty level (FPL). In Hancock and Harrison counties, the population was even

---

[1] Note that more stringent building-code standards were introduced in 1985. However, the U.S. Census Bureau, the source of our information, categorizes housing vintage on a decade-by-decade basis. We thus select 1980—as opposed to 1990—as the cutoff point, as most buildings constructed before this year would not have been built to the more-stringent codes.

Figure 3.1
SIL and 100-Year Flood Extent Overlay on Population Density of Coastal Mississippi

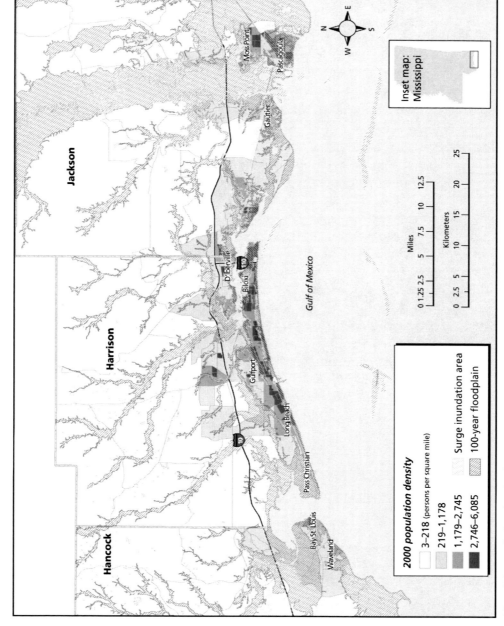

SOURCES: Population density data: U.S. Census Bureau (2000a). SIL November 2005: FEMA-provided flood advisory maps.
Floodplain data: FEMA (undated [a], 1998 series).
RAND OP162-3.1

worse off, with almost three-quarters of the housing units occupied by households making less than the median U.S. income level. This provides some insights into the magnitude of the affordable-housing challenge in this region, since a substantial portion of the prehurricane population earned relatively low incomes. Further county-by-county details are presented in the appendix.

As discussed earlier, it is generally difficult, for a variety of reasons, to replace affordable rental units following a natural disaster. Across the three-county area, almost 40 percent of the housing units were either rented or vacant. The lowest home-ownership rates occurred in the coastal communities of Harrison County, namely Gulfport and Biloxi. The low rates of home ownership in these areas, combined with the inherent difficulties in replenishing the stock of rental housing following natural disasters, suggest that the challenges of rebuilding affordable housing in coastal Mississippi will be particularly acute.

The vintage of the housing can also make a difference in the estimates and expectations for damage levels and rebuilding requirements. Homes designed prior to 1980 did not incorporate more-recent safety codes and housing-technology innovations—such as higher foundations and more wind-resistant wall panels and roofing systems—and as a result they were more susceptible to storm-related damages. Given the strength of the winds and the size of the storm surge, of course, even the most stringent building codes might not have been sufficient to prevent the leveling of homes and other structures located right along the coast. Further inland, however, the implementation of modern safety codes could account for the difference between moderate damage and total destruction.

Table 3.1 provides summary data on households and housing units located within the three coastal counties of Hancock, Harrison, and Jackson prior to Hurricane Katrina, along with estimates of the corresponding percentages exposed to flooding or the coastal surge during the storm. As the data indicate, these counties were characterized by high percentages of lower-income households, of rented or vacant homes, and of properties constructed prior to 1980.

Figure 3.2 presents a visual overlay of the storm-surge and flood zones and the percentage of the housing stock built prior to 1980. From the figure, it is clear that older homes were especially prevalent within the coastal cities of Harrison County (Gulfport and Biloxi) and Jackson County (Pascagoula and Moss Point) that suffered the brunt of the storm.

Table 3.1
Pre-Katrina Household and Housing Characteristics and Estimates of Katrina Damage Exposures

Characteristic	Pre-Katrina Characteristics	Percent Within Previous Flood Zone (FIRM) or Within SIL
Number of units	152,386	53
Household income		
<150% FPL	10%	6
<U.S. median income	66%	35
Rented or vacant	39%	22
Built before 1980	62%	36

Figure 3.2
SIL and 100-Year Flood Extent Overlay on Percent of Housing Units Built Before 1980 in Coastal Areas

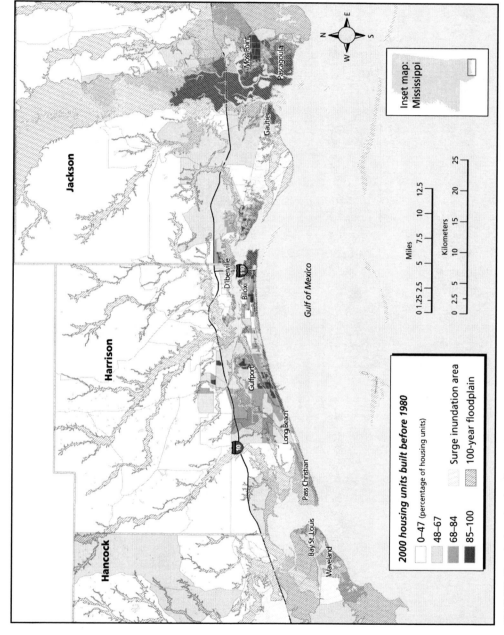

SOURCES: Population density data: U.S. Census Bureau (2000a). SIL November 2005: FEMA-provided flood advisory maps.
Floodplain data: FEMA (undated [a], 1998 series).

RAND OP162-3.2

Estimate of Surge and Flood Damage Exposures of Households

To develop a lower bound on the number of homes that were likely exposed to potential storm-related damage, we estimated the quantity of housing units within known flood zones (based on FEMA's FIRM maps) or within the storm surge zone (based on FEMA's SIL maps). We also estimated in greater detail the level of damage experienced on the peninsular tip of Biloxi.

Our findings indicate that about 40,000 housing units were located within the FIRM zones across the three-county area, and thus were potentially damaged by flooding. More than 75,000 units fell within the SIL area, and thus were potentially exposed to damage by the coastal surge. In total, more than 81,000 housing units were exposed to either flooding or the storm surge, and many of these were likely affected by both.[2] As indicated in Table 3.1, this represents more than half of the total housing stock within the three-county area.

Households living below the U.S. median household income level and exposed to flooding or surge damage occupied at least one-third of the housing units across the three counties. This means that at least 27,000 affordable-housing units will likely need to be replaced. These units, however, were not distributed equally in the three counties. Hancock County, where residents earning below the median income occupied more than half of the housing units, faces the steepest challenge in replenishing its stock of affordable housing.

Rented or vacant units exposed to flood or surge damage represented almost a quarter of the housing units (over 35,000 in total) across the three counties, with the highest share located in Hancock County. As discussed earlier, these units may be the most difficult to recover given that their owners may have less incentive to rebuild.

Finally, homes built prior to 1980 and located within the flood or surge zones represented more than one-third of the total housing stock within the three counties. These likely sustained the greatest damage.

Estimates of Damage Levels for Biloxi

To illustrate the type of thorough analysis that should be performed for the region once more comprehensive flooding and damage data become available, we conducted a more detailed damage assessment for the peninsular tip of Biloxi. Figures 3.3 and 3.4 illustrate the pattern of damage levels experienced in that area. Table 3.2 summarizes our estimates of the varying degrees of damage.

---

[2] Note again that we have not considered wind damage, and for other reasons described, these estimates likely underestimate overall damage exposure.

Figure 3.3
Residential Substantial Damage Estimate Equal-Damage Contours for Biloxi, Mississippi

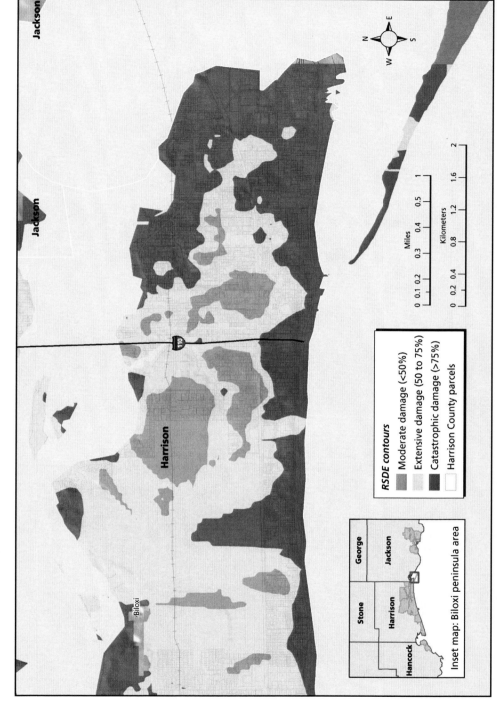

SOURCES: Residential Substantial Damage Estimate (RSDE) sample of approximately 2,600 units from FEMA, November 2005. RSDE contour layer compiled by the RAND Corporation.

RAND OP162-3.3

Figure 3.4
Ground Truth of RSDE Equal-Damage Contour Model

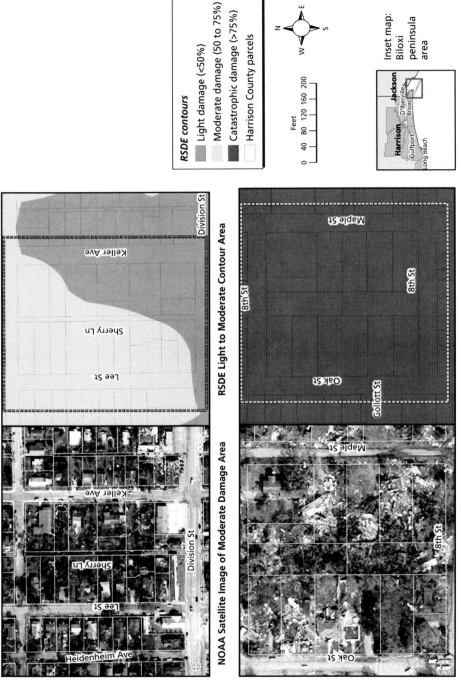

RAND OP162-3.4

Table 3.2
Pre-Katrina Household Characteristics and Modeled Damage Levels for Biloxi, Mississippi

Characteristic	Pre-Katrina	Extensively or Catastrophically Damaged
Housing units	6,400	5,130
Less than median income	6,000	4,800
Rented or vacant	3,900	3,100
Built before 1980	5,700	4,600

Figure 3.3 illustrates various damage levels, ranging from moderate to catastrophic, along the peninsular tip of Biloxi based on FEMA's Residential Substantial Damage Estimate (RSDE) data. Figure 3.4, in turn, offers a side-by-side comparison of on-the-ground damage as viewed through high-resolution satellite imagery and the damage categories represented within the RSDE data. The "catastrophic damage" contours, for instance, show all structures completely destroyed. In future analyses, satellite imagery can be merged with the RSDE data to verify damage levels throughout all of Mississippi, yielding information that will prove extremely useful in the local planning process for rebuilding and reconstruction.

As shown in Table 3.2, households living below the U.S. median income level occupied almost all the housing units within this small section of Biloxi, and about 80 percent of the housing units experienced extensive or catastrophic damage. More than 60 percent of housing units in this area were rented or vacant, and the vast majority of these were extensively or catastrophically damaged. Finally, about 90 percent of the housing units in this area were built before 1980, of which 73 percent of sustained extensive or catastrophic damage.

Conclusions

In all views—for the three counties as a whole, for each individual county, and for the Biloxi study area—we see that many of the areas hardest hit by Katrina were relatively densely populated, included large percentages of low-income households and had a high number of rental units. Given the lessons learned from previous disasters—in particular the difficulties associated with replenishing the stock of affordable housing—these findings indicate that there will be considerable challenges for rebuilding in these areas. According to our analysis, Gulfport and Biloxi (in Harrison County) and Pascagoula and Moss Point (in Jackson County) may face the steepest hurdles given that their residents have limited means to invest in the rebuilding effort and that their former lessors or investors may find it more financially attractive to rebuild elsewhere. Finally, many of the homes that were exposed to flooding and the coastal surge across the three counties were not built to current building codes and likely sustained the greatest damage.

CHAPTER FOUR

Options for Enhancing the Supply and Quality of Affordable Housing

Given the preliminary nature of the analysis performed for this report, RAND could not offer a definitive set of recommendations for addressing affordable-housing needs in coastal Mississippi following the destruction of Hurricane Katrina. Quite simply, more research is required to provide the best input to policy decisions. One area of open questions relates to the housing markets within the affected area. Coastal Mississippi comprises many local housing markets, some of which will be significantly stronger than others, and the need for intervention within strong housing markets may be very different from the need within weak ones. For example, if the reconstruction of market-rate housing does not have sufficient momentum on its own, will higher-income households bid up the price of the remaining lower-cost inventory? Will the reconstruction of market-rate housing require significant public intervention, and how will this affect the availability of resources for expanding the affordable housing stock? If there is not significant public underwriting of housing investments, is there momentum for private lending in market-rate housing?

Another important area for research is to develop a better understanding of the communities that have been displaced by Katrina. Exactly how many households were displaced, and how many of these were lower income? Did those displaced remain in the region or move to other locations? If they remained in the region, how are they currently meeting their housing needs? Has the reduced stock of affordable housing and the increased demand from displaced households increased the price level for the remaining stock of lower-cost housing? What types of assistance have been received from HUD and FEMA, and for how long will this assistance continue?

A third area of open questions pertains to the politics of housing. Policies to support affordable housing are typically established only when sufficient political pressure is applied, especially through organized groups dissatisfied with their housing choices. Following Katrina, are there enough low-income residents and advocates remaining in coastal Mississippi to participate in plans for housing redevelopment, to apply political pressure if the production of new, affordable units proceeds too slowly for them, and to ensure that the new housing serves their needs? If the devastation of low-income communities along the coast leads to a demographic shift toward a higher percentage of middle- and higher-income families, would these groups advocate for or against more affordable housing? Will the business community—to ensure an adequate workforce—lobby for affordable-housing options, or will many business owners simply choose to locate to other regions? Taking into consideration the fact that many of the recommendations offered in the wake of previous disasters such as Hurricane Camille never gained much traction or achieved long-term political follow-through, who will advocate for affordable-housing initiatives in Mississippi over the long term, long after elected officials have transitioned to other positions?

Clearly, the development of specific policy recommendations for an effective long-term affordable-housing strategy in Mississippi will be strongly influenced by the answers to questions such as these. Even so, it is possible at this point to offer a preliminary set of promising policy options that may help to enhance both the supply and the quality of affordable housing in the Gulf Coast communities as Mississippi rebuilds in the wake of Hurricane Katrina. Broadly, these options include further analyses (to address questions such as those discussed previously), pilot tests, regulatory and incentive-based policy options, institutional strategies and reforms, planning tools, private-sector initiatives, and innovative financial strategies. Drawing upon findings and observations from past studies within the affordable-housing and disaster-recovery literatures, the options presented here are divided into five broad categories related to (1) informing and overseeing long-term policy implementation; (2) increasing the supply and affordability of housing in both the short and long term; (3) building affordable housing to safer code standards; (4) fostering long-term affordability through lower life-cycle costs; and (5) enhancing local involvement in the planning and rebuilding process.

These categories are summarized in Table 4.1. The first column lists the categories of options presented within this paper, while the second and third columns present the relevant lessons learned from the affordable-housing and disaster-recovery literatures, respectively.

The specific options presented within each of these categories are discussed in greater detail within the following subsections.

Table 4.1
Policy Options Categories and Relevant Lessons Learned

Options Categories	Lessons from Affordable-Housing Literature	Lessons from Disaster-Recovery Literature
Informing and overseeing long-term policy implementation	Educate and inform low-income residents on funding opportunities and finance strategies	Provide information for decisionmaking Streamline the rebuilding and funding efforts Integrate the planning process
Increase the supply of affordable housing Reduce the costs of affordable housing	Factor financial need into the distribution of funds Engage in post-disaster planning to identify the scope of needs	
Building affordable housing to safer code standards	Increase the quality of affordable housing	Rebuild with higher safety standards to mitigate future problems
Fostering long-term affordability	Reduce the long-term costs of affordable housing, including maintenance and utilities	Develop strategies to encourage the development of efficient and durable homes
Enhancing local involvement in the planning and rebuilding process	Involve the community in affordable-housing advocacy	Involve the community in planning and rebuilding efforts

Options to Inform and Oversee Long-Term Policy Solutions

The options within this section are intended to ensure that the information necessary to inform long-term policy choices is available to decisionmakers and that the institutional capacity to oversee and evaluate the long-term solutions is developed. As we have seen in previous examples of post-disaster planning, it is difficult for policymakers to develop robust, practical, and effective policies without access to timely and reliable information on the scope and the scale of the challenges to be addressed. At the same time, there must be institutions in place to leverage this information and coordinate planning efforts effectively.

Perform Research on Three Key Questions to Inform Long-Term Policy

Long-term planning for affordable housing in Mississippi will likely involve a portfolio of policy options. It will also require interactions between federal, state, and local officials, builders and developers, employers, and citizens. To identify the most effective set of policies to implement, decisionmakers must first gain deeper insight into three critical questions:

- What are the long-term housing needs?
- What are the barriers to ensuring an adequate supply of affordable housing?
- Which best practices from around the country can be applied in Mississippi?

Individually, each of these questions is important; together, they provide the base of information that will enable policymakers to identify and select the most effective and robust long-term policy options. Below, we describe in greater detail the type of research that will be needed to answer these questions.

What are the long-term housing needs? The general goals of a housing needs assessment study would be to determine the number of housing units that were damaged or destroyed, to evaluate the demographic characteristics of the displaced population, to determine the number and geographic distribution of housing units at different price points that will need to be rebuilt in order to meet the needs of displaced residents and local businesses, to develop an estimate of the costs of rebuilding, and to identify sources of financial support such as insurance payments, private loans, and state and federal relief funds that can support the rebuilding efforts. Information would need to be gathered on a county-by-county and community-by-community basis, and it would be correlated with financial data, planned infrastructure projects, case-management information, and other planning concerns to help guide state and federal funding efforts in the most productive manner. The study would focus on the following factors:

- Demographics information about the displaced residents, including their incomes, their household characteristics, where they lived, and where they went following the storm
- Details about the pre-Katrina housing stock, including vintage, type, ownership, and replacement value
- The relationships between housing damages, household demographics, aid received thus far, and aid still needed

- Identification of current housing shortages, categorized by type (e.g., single-family versus multifamily housing), by income level (e.g., affordable to middle-income, to low-income, or to very low-income households), and by region
- Estimates of the near- and long-term employment opportunities in different communities and the associated implications for housing needs over different time horizons
- Information about suitable sites for redevelopment
- Estimates of what it will cost to rebuild the housing stock, as well as the approximate percentages that may be covered by borrowing, by insurance, and by government recovery funds
- Information about the logistical challenges associated with rebuilding, including the flows of materials, workers, and residents
- An understanding of the coordination that will be required between housing redevelopment and other infrastructure improvement projects
- Potential strategies for integrating the outputs from local design charrettes into the housing redevelopment planning efforts
- Estimates of the costs and benefits of various affordable-housing policy options offered by the Mississippi Governor's Commission on Recovery, Rebuilding, Renewal.

Conducting such an assessment represents a critical precursor for the development of long-term policy strategies capable of addressing Mississippi's formidable affordable-housing challenges.

What are the barriers to ensuring an adequate supply of affordable housing? The purpose of this assessment would be to identify any factors that could inhibit the construction of a sufficient supply of safe, efficient, and affordable housing. Specific issues to be examined would include:

- Existing code and zoning provisions within individual counties and cities in the affected region that could restrict the types of housing that can be built
- The capacity of local agencies to enforce new policies and oversee new construction
- The existing institutional framework and the manner in which housing-related policy decisions are made.

This information would be used to assess the barriers that could restrict the supply of affordable housing in communities where lower-income workers are employed. Specific findings could indicate opportunities for legislative action at the state level (for example, requiring all counties and municipalities to embed certain provisions within their zoning ordinances), or they could suggest beneficial actions on the part of individual local governments (for example, removing code restrictions within a city that prevent the use of modular housing technologies).

Which best practices from around the country can be applied in Mississippi? The primary aims within this study would be to identify and assess alternatives and best practices in the areas of building-safety codes, building-efficiency technologies, zoning and land-use strategies, and community design principles. As communities throughout the Gulf Coast begin the process of planning and rebuilding following the hurricanes, they will need to make a variety of important choices that will heavily influence both the short- and long-term outcomes for the renewal efforts. Should stricter building-safety codes be mandated at the state or local level? Should incentive structures be put into place to encourage developers and builders to construct more resource-efficient homes that lower the life-cycle costs for owners and tenants? Should communities employ zoning strategies that allow for dense, mixed-use development patterns to create more vibrant urban neighborhoods and foster greater opportunities for walking, biking, and transit? The information derived through this study would help decisionmakers identify the different options that are possible and determine those that would be most appropriate in various Gulf Coast communities.

In the aftermath of Hurricane Katrina, decisionmakers have a unique opportunity to learn from the best practices of other communities, as well as to take advantage of existing federal government programs that can assist in technology options and planning. With respect to the question of safety, Florida's building codes for hurricane-prone areas may offer useful guidance for Mississippi, and California's experience in designing safety codes for earthquake resistance may also yield valuable lessons. For the question of resource efficiency, the energy building codes of California and New York provide potentially useful models, and the U.S. Environmental Protection Agency (EPA) ENERGY STAR® program and various U.S. Department of Energy (DOE) building programs also offer a wealth of ideas and technical expertise. Finally, in the area of land-use planning and community design, the evolving paradigms of smart growth and new urbanism suggest a variety of strategies for integrating the goals of economic growth, social equity, and environmental protection.

By evaluating technology and policy approaches from other areas of the country and adopting those that are most appropriate in Mississippi, federal, state, and local decisionmakers involved in the renewal effort can profoundly influence the long-term outcomes in local communities. Homes can be made safer in the event of future disasters, homes can be designed to be more durable and resource-efficient to reduce the life-cycle costs for owners and tenants, and neighborhoods can be structured to encourage local economic development, social cohesion, and environmental integrity. To support these goals, the proposed study would identify and evaluate a range of relevant technology and policy alternatives, focusing in particular on their costs and benefits as well as their applicability to the Gulf Coast region. Specific areas to be addressed would include the following:

- Technologies for greater wind and flood resistance
- Technologies for reducing maintenance requirements and using water and energy more efficiently
- Building codes to mandate minimum safety or efficiency requirements
- Incentive programs to encourage the development of safer or more-efficient buildings
- Building inspection management practices
- Zoning, land-use, and urban-design strategies.

Develop the Capability to Oversee, Coordinate, and Manage Affordable-Housing Rebuilding Efforts

To ensure that recovery funds and rebuilding efforts are channeled efficiently and equitably, it may be appropriate for the state to establish an institution capable of overseeing the long-term planning and policy efforts in the area of affordable housing. Critical roles for this institution would include implementing recommendations in the Governor's Commission report, coordinating funding from a diverse set of sources and channeling support to specific projects, providing information to low-income households about different financial resources and programs available, and providing best-practice guidelines and planning options to local communities. While the institution would initially focus on housing recovery challenges in the aftermath of Hurricane Katrina, over time, it could evolve to support longer-range statewide affordable-housing goals.

One option would be to structure this institution as a statewide, private, nonprofit "community development entity" (CDE), following the model used for the Arizona Neighborhood Economic Development Corporation (AHC, 2002). The CDC would then be granted responsibility for the following:

- *Oversight of the housing recovery efforts.* This would include supervising the implementation of policy options suggested in the Governor's Commission report.
- *Funding coordination and management.* This would involve identifying, collecting, prioritizing, and disbursing available funds for the development and renewal of affordable housing, factoring in considerations related to need and equity. Specific tasks related to this role might include the following:
  - Coordinating different public funding mechanisms (such as HUD funds, low-income tax credits, and new market tax credits) and facilitating the flow of resources from state and federal agencies to the projects for which they are most needed
  - Coordinating the funds and efforts offered by philanthropic and NGO programs concerned with housing issues such as Habitat for Humanity or the Enterprise Foundation
  - Developing clear criteria for prioritizing the disbursal of funds to affordable-housing projects, which might include local demographic factors, business employment needs, safety and efficiency considerations, and consistency with intended design guidelines
  - Ensuring that lower-income representatives and local affordable-housing advocates have a "seat at the table" to advise on the disbursement of funding and the design for specific projects
  - Coordinating the participation of various entities—public, private, and nonprofit— within specific projects.
- *Outreach and education.* Many aspects of the rebuilding process will be either financially complex or technically novel. For instance, specific projects may involve leveraging public and private funds for affordable-housing development, or they may require the application and permitting of new safety, efficiency, or design guidelines. For this reason, the

entity should be capable of offering educational outreach on a variety of issues to residents, developers, and communities. Specific educational outreach roles could include the following:

- Developing financial-literacy programs to help residents and builders understand financial opportunities that are available for affordable housing. Challenges such as preexisting credit problems, income disruptions, and existing mortgages on damaged or destroyed properties will create roadblocks for families trying to put their lives back together. Under such circumstances, families will be prime targets for predatory lending offers promising an easy way out. A major initiative will therefore be needed to help arm families against this problem. Ideally, this initiative would involve credit counselors, qualified loan staff from banks and mortgage companies, housing counselors, community action agencies, Mississippi Cooperative Extension agents, and contractors from FEMA's United Methodist Committee on Relief (UMCOR) and National Voluntary Organizations Active in Disaster (NVOAD) programs. What is needed is a flexible and sophisticated assistance and advisory system to help steer families in need away from deleterious financial decisions. Many organizations that could play a valuable role in this undertaking already exist in Mississippi, but the effectiveness of their efforts could be enhanced through increased coordination.

- Providing "best practices" guidelines for various building technologies designed to make homes safer and more efficient

- Reviewing design options that support more walkable and vibrant communities (this could include coordination with any established "regional design centers," such as the pilot design center project proposed by the Enterprise Foundation).

- *Coordination of regional planning efforts.* To maximize the effectiveness and efficiency of Mississippi's rebuilding and renewal efforts, housing decisions should be coordinated with infrastructure planning (including, for instance, transportation, waterworks, and sewage). Over the short term, the CDE could take efforts to ensure that affordable-housing development activities are coordinated with other infrastructure investments throughout coastal Mississippi. Over the longer term, a regional planning entity might be formed to assume this role.

The CDE might also include advisory boards staffed by community representatives from different counties and cities within the state who could provide input on local priorities. In its early years of operation, the bulk of the funding could be directed to affordable-housing projects within the devastated coastal counties. Over the long run, however, as coastal restoration progresses, the CDE could devote an increasing share of funding to selected affordable-housing projects in other areas of the state.

Options to Increase the Supply and Affordability of Housing in the Near Term and Long Term

Prior to Hurricane Katrina, the coastal region of Mississippi already faced significant challenges related to affordable housing. With the widespread destruction caused by flooding, surge, and wind damages, these existing problems have been greatly exacerbated. To make matters worse, many of the displaced families from coastal Mississippi come from lower-income groups, and many of the jobs in the area pay comparatively low wages. At the same time, new investment in the region following Hurricane Katrina may very well lead to an increase in local land values.

Against this backdrop, it is critical to identify a set of strategies that will speed the redevelopment of a sufficient supply of affordable housing in the near term, and that will ensure that the stock of affordable housing does not decline in future years. To meet these goals, it will be useful to approach the problem from several angles:

- It will be important to take steps to ensure that affordable housing is constructed where it is most needed—in the communities where lower-income people live and work.
- Given the magnitude of the post-Katrina affordable-housing gap, a significant and reliable source of housing subsidization funds likely will be required over a prolonged period.
- It may be possible to leverage innovative designs and financial strategies to lower the costs of affordable housing.
- There may be opportunities to promote home ownership among lower-income families who formerly relied on rental housing.
- It will be critical to pursue strategies designed to ensure that the stock of developed affordable rental and ownership units developed over the near term remain affordable over the long term.

Collectively, the options provided within this section offer the potential to address these different aspects of the challenge.

Establish Permanent Affordability Goals

In developing affordable housing, policymakers may wish to consider the proximity of the units to job opportunities available to workers with lower skill sets. This importance of this issue is underscored by the fact that the percentage of individuals who are unable or cannot afford to drive is much higher among lower-income groups than within the population as a whole (Blumenberg, 2003). One option for achieving a better balance between low-wage jobs and affordable housing would be to encourage local governments to set and maintain permanent affordable-housing goals (also referred to as "regional fair share housing"; Katz et al., 2003). For instance, the requirements might specify that 50 percent of the low-wage earners in a community should have access to affordable housing within that community. Specific affordability goals on a community-by-community basis would be determined through an in-depth housing and business needs assessment, and incentives could be created to encourage local governments to develop plans for achieving their affordability goals. For example, the state could be responsible for programmatic oversight, and it could encourage compliance among local jurisdictions by withholding state or federal redevelopment funds from communities that fail to develop realistic affordable-housing plans. This would be similar, for example, to the arrangement in which states are required to generate plans for meeting ambient air quality standards specified under the Clean Air Act in order to receive certain federal transportation funds (Environmental Defense, 2001).

Establish State and Local Housing Trust Funds

Identifying a sufficient and reliable source of public subsidy funds is undoubtedly the most daunting challenge to rebuilding an adequate supply of affordable housing within coastal Mississippi. Regrettably, much of the money would need to be raised at the state or local levels, at least if past trends in the federal government continue. According to a recent report issued by the National Low Income Housing Coalition, for instance, the total federal budget authority (in 2004 adjusted dollars) for low-income housing program outlays between 1976 and 2004 declined by 59 percent (Dolbeare, Saraf, and Crowley, 2004). With the current magnitude of the federal budget deficit, this trend promises to continue in the foreseeable future.

To offset the decline in federal funding for low-income housing, an increasing number of states and localities have established housing trust funds (Brooks, 1999, 2002; Center for Community Change, undated), a powerful and flexible method of dedicating public money to the creation and preservation of affordable housing. First created in the mid-1970s, housing trust funds became more common throughout the late 1980s and 1990s as the availability of federal funds dwindled. As of late 2005, more than 400 state and local housing trust funds had been established within the United States. None of these, however, is located in Mississippi.

Housing trust funds are distinct accounts that receive dedicated sources of public funds to support various activities associated with affordable housing, including new construction, rehabilitation, rental assistance, and homeless shelters. They are typically established through state legislation or local ordinances that (1) create the fund; (2) establish an administrative structure for overseeing its operation; (3) specify regulatory requirements that govern the expenditure of the funds; and (4) identify the source of public funds that will be dedicated to the trust (Brooks, 2002).

In practice, housing trust funds have leveraged a wide array of revenue streams, including:

- Property transactions, such as taxes on real estate transfers or interest on pooled escrow accounts
- Development charges, such as taxes on new development, payments for density bonuses, or taxes on the conversion of rental units to condos
- Municipal taxes, such as sales taxes, property taxes, hotel room taxes, and tax increments from redevelopment zones
- Government activities, such as proceeds from the sale of publicly owned land, repayments from government loan programs, or fees from landfill activities
- Bond programs, such as funds from government bonds, surplus from bond refinancing, or fees from bond-financed programs

- Other miscellaneous sources, such as taxes on lottery earning, contributions from employers, or interest from tenant security deposits.

Given such funds' power to provide much-needed revenues to support affordable housing, Mississippi could reap considerable benefits from the establishment of a statewide housing trust fund. Possible revenue sources to consider include proceeds from retail activities (e.g., sales taxes), tourism (e.g., hotel taxes or restaurant taxes), gambling (e.g., gaming license fees or taxes on gambling winnings), or oil-production activities. Such sources offer two compelling advantages. First, they are capable of providing a significant and reliable level of funding on a year-to-year basis. Second, they involve industries that require a significant share of lower-income employees, providing a compelling rationale to channel a portion of their proceeds to support affordable housing.

In addition to creating a state-level housing trust fund, Mississippi might also consider passing legislation that would encourage counties and cities to create local-level trust funds, a step that has already been taken in Missouri, New Jersey, Pennsylvania, and Washington. For example, in 1993, the Washington legislature passed an act that allows counties, cities, and towns to exceed statutory property tax limitations for the purpose of financing affordable housing for very low-income households (Brooks, 2002). For coastal Mississippi, where a substantial amount of rebuilding will be required, allowing local jurisdictions to set aside a portion of tax increment finance revenues in redevelopment zones to be dedicated to affordable housing could provide an effective strategy.

Though these ideas offer considerable potential over the longer term, they are unlikely to generate significant revenues for affordable housing for at least several years. Consider, for instance, that the property-tax bases in the cities and counties most affected by Hurricane Katrina have been destroyed, while the tourism and gaming industries are likewise still in shambles. As such, it is also important to identify options for securing funding in the nearer term, as well as to evaluate strategies for leveraging existing resources as efficiently as possible.

Encourage Employer-Based Housing Assistance

Another potential source of funding, one that could be leveraged in the nearer term, is private firms located within Mississippi. Though employers do not have a legal responsibility to assist their employees with affordable-housing options, in many circumstances it may be in their best interest to do so. This is especially true for post-Katrina Mississippi, where the lack of affordable housing may severely curtail the available labor pool as businesses attempt to rebuild. Given the inevitable links between housing and workforce issues, it may be advantageous to seek the financial assistance of employers in rebuilding the affordable-housing stock in coastal Mississippi. This task could potentially be championed by the CDE discussed under "Develop the Capability to Oversee, Coordinate, and Manage Affordable-Housing Rebuilding Efforts." To implement this suggestion, the CDE would (1) help educate businesses on the advantages of providing financial assistance to support affordable housing (note that many of these advantages would be more fully articulated based on the results of the housing needs assessment under "Perform Research on Three Key Questions to Inform Long-Term Policy"); and (2) create the appropriate institutional mechanisms to funnel corporate housing assistance in the most efficient manner. One possible channel for employer-assisted affordable-housing aid could be through community land trusts, as discussed under "Create Community Land Trusts for Long-Term Affordable Ownership Units." Another idea would be for employers to help moderate- and low-income workers with home-buying assistance in the form of a grant or forgivable loan that could be used for the down payment or closing costs on a home purchase (often referred to as employer-assisted housing, or EAH; Jennings, 2000). Note that, in the case, of the gambling industry, Mississippi's gaming act requires peripheral community investments by casinos. Given the current magnitude of the housing shortage, the state might consider allowing investments in affordable housing to qualify as meeting this regulation.

Set Affordability Requirements or Incentives for Developers

Although local governments can develop plans to meet affordable-housing needs, developers will ultimately provide the housing. Recognizing this link, it may be appropriate to set up programs that either require or provide incentives for developers to include affordable housing units within their projects (commonly referred to as "developer set-asides"; Katz et al., 2003). One possible implementation of this strategy would be to mandate that developers, as part of the permitting process, create a minimum percentage of affordable housing within any new development plan (the specific percentage selected could depend on the targets described under "Establish Permanent Affordability Goals"). As an alternative to providing affordable housing within a specific project, developers could also be granted the option of paying "in lieu" fees that would accrue to the community's affordable-housing fund (these might, for example, be channeled into a community land trust, as described under "Create Community Land Trusts for Long-Term Affordable Ownership Units"). This approach could be adopted on a community-by-community basis, as part of a local government's plan for providing its fair share of affordable housing.

In place of, or in addition to, affordability requirements for developers, cities and counties could also create incentives to encourage developers to incorporate a greater percentage of affordable housing within their projects (as well as to make their housing units safer and more efficient). These incentives could take the form of density bonuses (allowing higher densities than would normally be allowed within the zoning requirements), expedited permitting, waived or reduced off-street parking requirements, or other incentives backed by financial mechanisms (Katz et al., 2003). These may be less controversial than affordability requirements for developers, and thus could potentially be instituted more rapidly. Putting such programs into place early could stimulate the development of more affordable housing as the rebuilding process begins.

Adopt Zoning Codes That Support Dense, Mixed-Use Development

Where policymakers want to create vibrant neighborhoods that support affordable-housing goals and enable residents to make more of their journeys by foot, by bike, or by transit, communities will benefit by adopting zoning codes that allow for dense, mixed-use development, including ample multifamily housing. This may be especially relevant for housing sites on government property, where the public land ownership provides an immediate, deep subsidy for affordable housing. Commonly cited zoning options in this vein include reducing the minimum footprint for lots, increasing the allowable floor-area ratio, reducing or elimi-nating required property setbacks, reducing off-street parking requirements, allowing shorter driveways or smaller garages, allowing accessory units, and permitting multiple uses (e.g., apartments above ground-floor retail) on individual parcels (Arigoni, 2001; Katz et al., 2003; Litman, 2005; Shoup, 2005). Without doubt, pursuing these alternatives may, in certain cases, involve significant restructuring of existing zoning practices. There are, however, successful precedents for rezoning in the wake of other natural disasters in the nation's history (Schwab, 1998).

One of the most likely barriers to implementing dense, mixed-use zoning strategies is the potential for existing homeowner groups to adopt a "not in my backyard" (NIMBY) stance toward affordable housing (Luger and Temkin, 2000; May, 2005). In particular, it is common for single-family housing neighborhoods to protest against higher densities or multiple-family housing, fearing that such changes would lead to greater traffic congestion or reduced property values. Considering the magnitude of the current housing crisis in Mississippi, however, afford-able apartments will need to be a part of the solution. After all, not all families will be able to achieve home ownership, and it will not be financially feasible to build an adequate stock of affordable rental units in scattered, single-family home developments. Fortunately, investing in smart growth principles such as greater density, mixed-use patterns, and improved transit can in fact *increase* the desirability and cohesion of neighborhoods (Litman, 2005). Therefore, educating local communities on these benefits and providing concrete examples of the success-ful application of smart growth principles in other communities may help to short-circuit the potential for NIMBY attitudes in the Mississippi rebuilding process.

Pilot a Public-Private Partnership to Develop Mixed-Income Housing on a HUD Site

According to the Mississippi HUD office, Katrina damaged more than 3,000 subsidized rental units. These rental units provided housing for some of the poorest families on the coast, includ-ing elderly, disabled, and other renters on very low fixed incomes. Local housing authorities owned and managed most of these units. The Waveland Housing Authority, for example, owned and managed 75 units that were all destroyed in the hurricane. The question that now must be addressed is whether to rebuild these affordable-housing developments as they were or redesign them.

One of the common challenges with low-income housing developments is that they are often located in relative isolation. This pattern may inadvertently create segregated low-income clusters that find it difficult to integrate with other segments of a community. Instead of creat-ing new housing projects with one level of income-accessible housing, a more promising strat-egy might be to create mixed-income housing communities in which lower-income units are intermixed with middle- or upper-middle units. Loukaitou-Sideris and Kamel (2004) empha-size the potential benefits of developing pilots to test innovative options such as this.

The goal of the pilot proposed in this option would be to start with a former HUD housing site that was destroyed during the hurricane and develop a new high-density, mixed-income, affordable-housing project. Rather than rebuilding HUD housing by itself on this site, public and private partners would join together to design and implement a mixed-income neighborhood. The pilot project could combine best practices from recent HUD projects along with relevant "smart growth" or "new urbanism" elements. This partnership could be formed in a way that spreads the risk and, at the same time, leverages both public and private moneys in a way that could not occur if each of the neighborhoods were to be developed separately. The main challenge in developing such a project would be to make sure that there was no net loss in the number of dwelling units that are affordable to very low-income households.

Offer a Private Finance Initiative

Given the sheer scope of the affordable-housing crisis in Mississippi in the wake of Katrina, it is unlikely that public coffers, either at the state or federal levels, can offer sufficient capital resources to finance an adequate supply of affordable units. For this reason, it may be beneficial to pursue opportunities to leverage private sources of capital. One promising option for engaging private capital may be through the use of private finance initiatives, or PFI (Akintoye, Beck, and Hardcastle, 2003; Yescombe, 2002). Under the PFI paradigm, the government provides an annuity stream to private concerns to help them undertake projects that would not otherwise be profitable. For example, a development firm might construct affordable housing and collect below-market rents from residents and then be eligible for a supplemental payment directly from the government designed to keep the rents affordable. This type of program could potentially be supported by federal, state, and local governments, and it would also be possible to develop an endowment for this purpose combining public, philanthropic, and private money.

Offer Subsidized Mortgages to Qualified Individuals

As Mississippi residents struggle to rebuild in the wake of Hurricane Katrina, existing mortgage programs will serve some, but not all, of the displaced population. Insurance settlements can be held up for FEMA resolutions, which have taken as long as 36 months in past situations, and SBA programs may not cover the full replacement or repair costs. This option would involve the development of mortgage programs to support segments of the population expected to encounter difficulty in recovering their pre-Katrina housing situation. These include elderly homeowners on fixed incomes who experienced severe loss, homeowners with mortgages whose settlements do not leave them with enough resources to rebuild without filing bankruptcy, and individuals whose credit is too poor to allow them to qualify for SBA funding.

Many low-income homeowners are likely to be uninsured or underinsured, while renters generally have limited cash for down payments. In addition, borrowers will face difficulty meeting traditional mortgage criteria due to hurricane-related issues such as unsettled insurance claims on existing mortgages or late payments due to income disruption. Even people with strong credit may lose their homes due to the inability to pay simultaneously for an existing mortgage on a damaged property, for temporary housing, and for rebuilding costs to either replace or repair damaged property. The flooding caused by the hurricanes in nonflood zones, where flood insurance was almost nonexistent, has only exacerbated problems. Nonpredatory mortgage products with flexible underwriting features, which take into account a borrower's prehurricane credit history and factor in other effects of the disaster, could ensure that low-income individuals and families are able to participate in the long-term recovery of their communities. Those facing mortgage defaults or foreclosure or those who have no other means to purchase a home could use these products.

One way to address this complex problem is to develop a subsidized mortgage product with below-market interest rates. To illustrate the importance of this option, Table 4.2 shows the interest rates that would be required at different loan amounts to make comparably affordable monthly payments.

As Table 4.2 shows, with lower interest rates, one could finance a $75,000 to $100,000 mortgage with a monthly payment of about $400 per month. However, finding a lender who will provide a mortgage with an interest rate below 6 percent is unlikely. A possible solution would be to set up a federal mortgage pool that would allow low- to moderate-income home buyers in the disaster area to obtain financing with below-market interest rates. This would help to deliver a superior product with monthly payments within the means of low- to moderate-income groups.

Table 4.2
Comparable Monthly Payments for 30-Year Loans at Different Loan Amounts and Interest Rates

Loan Amount ($K)	Interest Rate (%)	Monthly Payment ($)
100	2.5	395.12
75	5.0	402.62
65	6.0	389.71
50	8.5	384.46

Create Community Land Trusts for Long-Term Affordable Ownership Units

As communities strive to provide an adequate supply of affordable housing, one of their challenges will be to ensure that units initially developed to be affordable do, in fact, remain affordable over time. This is particularly relevant for coastal Mississippi, where new investment following Hurricane Katrina may raise land values above their prior levels. A promising approach to this challenge is to pool public and private funds to create community land trusts (CLTs) that maintain land for affordable housing ownership opportunities. A CLT is commonly structured as a nonprofit entity that owns the land but not the buildings on the land. Residents own the buildings themselves, have a long-term lease on the land, and act as members of the trust. The compelling advantage for CLTs is that they can be structured with "limited equity" or "shared appreciation mortgage" policies and formulas that restrict the resale price of the housing within the trust in order to maintain long-term affordability (Peterson, 1996).

To implement these trusts, local governments would work with housing advocacy groups to set up nonprofit CLT entities. Possible mechanisms for assembling CLTs would include land purchases, transferable development rights, land swaps, or eminent domain. If they are to be pursued, such steps should be pursued in the near term, while the destruction remains widespread and land values are relatively cheap. If necessary, the state could provide enabling legislation to govern various facets of the CLT institutional structure.

Leverage Nonprofit Ownership for Long-Term Affordable Rental Units

Government investment in subsidized rental housing often occurs in ways that do not ensure long-term affordability. One of the challenges in this area is that much of the subsidized stock has "expiring use" contracts that enable property owners to opt out of rental price restrictions in future years. A potential strategy for circumventing this problem would be to encourage nonprofit ownership structures for government-subsidized affordable rental housing developments. Nonprofit organizations, after all, are less likely to opt out of their subsidy arrangements because it would jeopardize their charter as public purpose entities. One way that this could be achieved would be for the statewide CDE suggested under "Develop the Capability to Oversee, Coordinate, and Manage Affordable-Housing Rebuilding Efforts" to give preferential funding access to affordable rental property proposals submitted by nonprofit organizations. The goal of long-term affordability for rental units may also be strengthened through the use of subordinate financing arrangements backed by long-term regulatory controls.

Options to Encourage Safe and Healthy Affordable Housing

In their efforts to reduce the cost of affordable housing, developers may be tempted to cut corners on the quality of construction. In other cases, low-income residents may not be armed with the information they need to make sure that construction is performed adequately. Yet while subpar quality may reduce the upfront costs of housing, it undoubtedly increases the safety risks and financial burden faced by low-income homeowners over the longer term, especially in areas prone to natural disasters such as hurricanes. In the face of severe flooding or high-velocity winds, substandard housing may sustain much higher levels of damage, posing unwarranted danger to the occupants and resulting in larger repair costs. Recognizing these elevated risks, insurance companies are also likely to charge higher premiums for substandard housing. To prevent such problems in future years, policymakers may adopt strategies during the redevelopment process to ensure that new housing is built to meet or exceed minimum construction-quality standards. To promote residents' health and well-being further, communities can take proactive steps to prevent the reconstruction of affordable housing in inappropriate locations, such as areas subject to higher levels of air and noise pollution from adjacent industrial or commercial operations.

The following options would increase the likelihood that the development of new affordable housing in coastal Mississippi would meet or exceed minimum safety standards, and that it would not be located in areas subject to flooding or high winds or within neighborhoods plagued by unhealthy levels of air pollution or noise pollution from nearby industrial operations.

Establish Strict Temporary Codes

While Hurricane Katrina struck with devastating power, it would appear that substandard building codes and questionable zoning practices in certain areas exacerbated the destruction. Prior to rebuilding, policymakers could address these gaps—now apparent in hindsight—to minimize the damage that may result from any future severe weather event to strike the coast. In fact, Mississippi Governor Haley Barbour has stated this as a priority (Pender, 2005). It may take some time, however, for cities and counties to evaluate and approve new building codes, and for FEMA to create new official base flood elevation maps indicating areas in which development is not advisable. Until these processes are completed, cities and counties might consider the idea of adopting strict temporary codes to ensure that buildings constructed during the near term meet basic minimum safety requirements. The interim codes could, for example, combine FEMA's interim base flood elevation advisories (FEMA, 2006) with Florida's stringent coastal hurricane-resistance building standards. Under these codes, homeowners or developers meeting the strict interim requirements would be allowed to rebuild as quickly as they would like, and their buildings would be grandfathered into any longer-term code programs. Homeowners and developers unwilling to meet the stringent temporary codes, on the other hand, would not be issued permits until longer-term codes have been instituted.

Set Minimum Long-Term Safety Codes

Over the longer term, cities and counties could establish stringent minimum building-safety codes based on the latest Southern Building Code (Southern Building Code Congress, undated) and International Building Code (International Code Council et al., undated) standards as well as hurricane- and flood-resistance codes. As noted earlier, one of the keys to rebuilding affordable housing that meets long-term needs is to anticipate potential problems in the future (Comerio, 1998). Instituting sufficiently stringent building codes can certainly be achieved at the city and county level, but to ensure conformity, it may be appropriate to establish and enforce such codes at the state level. Assuming that cities and counties adopt conservative temporary building codes over the short term, these permanent code changes can be adopted over a longer time frame, on the order of six months to a year. An example from the state of Florida illustrates the benefits of this approach. In 1994, following the devastation of Hurricane Andrew, Florida instituted statewide minimum building codes for coastal areas prone to hurricane damage, codes that were subsequently updated in 2002 and again in 2005. Following the series of hurricanes that struck the state in 2004, researchers at the University of Florida demonstrated that homes built after the code upgrade in 2002 sustained less damage than did those built according to the earlier 1994 codes, which, in turn, suffered much less damage than did homes built prior to 1994 (Dobson, 2004).

Develop Codes for Modular Housing

New modular housing technologies (in contrast to older "manufactured" housing) can be used to create homes that are attractive, affordable, and capable of meeting appropriate safety standards in hurricane-prone areas (Phillips, 2005). To leverage these potential advantages, cities and counties should consider reviewing their building codes to make sure that modular housing technologies are permissible within their jurisdictions. It may also be appropriate to reduce permit or inspection fees for modular housing because the burden on inspectors should be substantially less. Greater utilization of modular housing may also present an opportunity for economic development because modular-housing factories could be created in communities that require significant levels of rebuilding.

Because many communities have a negative impression of modular housing, it may be prudent to develop a pilot project to demonstrate the potential opportunities. One option would be to create a permanent modular-housing development on a site currently being used for transitional housing. Such a pilot program would serve two purposes. First, it would show how modular-housing technologies could be used to develop affordable, attractive, and efficient housing. To ease concerns over the quality and aesthetics of modular housing, this pilot would allow developers to compete for the chance to design and build homes within a mixed-use affordable-housing development to showcase the quality that can be achieved with modular technology. Based on the results of the competition, multiple modular-home developers could be selected to construct different parts of the pilot project.

The pilot's other purpose would be to identify transitional housing sites (possibly including trailer parks) that may be appropriate for permanent affordable housing. Given that money is being spent to lay infrastructure in these transitional sites, it would be wasteful simply to remove the infrastructure when the transitional housing is no longer needed. Along these lines, the pilot would be used to help identify appropriate criteria for identifying candidate sites and to develop processes for making the transition from temporary to permanent housing (with set-asides for affordable housing). Based on results of a successful pilot program, communities along the coast may feel more comfortable adopting codes to allow for modular-housing technologies, and it may be possible to convert a larger number of transitional sites from temporary to permanent housing developments.

Regulate the "Shadow" Housing Market

In areas where there is an insufficient supply of affordable housing, low-income residents may be forced to overcrowd the available stock, creating a shadow market that involves renting garages and building illegal additions. To promote the safety and welfare of their residents, local jurisdictions could attempt to legalize and regulate such activities. For example, in dealing with overcrowded conditions in a lower-income, single-family home neighborhood, a city might amend the zoning laws to allow for the addition of second units or "granny flats" and bring these into the permitting process.

Prevent Inappropriate Zoning

The current vision for redevelopment in Mississippi calls for increased airport capacity and the development of an inland port. However, along with their economic benefits, these land uses generate numerous negative externalities such as noise and air pollution and heavy truck traffic. As a result, land values surrounding such areas may decrease. However, policymakers should avoid the temptation to create affordable housing on land where the value has decreased for these reasons. Simply stated, the noise and air pollution would be harmful to any nearby residents, especially children (Bailey et al., 2004). Moreover, past experience from other areas in the county demonstrates that residents living near such facilities are often able to organize effectively against future facility expansion plans (e.g., Schoch, 2004). Areas near the airport or inland port should therefore be strictly zoned for compatible industrial or commercial purposes only.

Options to Increase Long-Term Affordability Through Lower Life-Cycle Costs

Providing housing that is affordable to lower-income workers involves not only making sure there is a sufficient supply, but also making sure that the housing has low life-cycle costs over the long run. In many cases, so-called affordable housing is extremely inefficient, and, as a result, residents must spend more on energy, utilities, and maintenance than residents of larger, more expensive homes. The overarching goal of the options in this section is to encourage builders and consumers to consider the long-run operational costs of a home—including safety risks, maintenance costs, water and energy costs, and transportation costs—in their development and purchase decisions.

In practice, builders often seek to reduce the costs of affordable housing by installing low-efficiency equipment, reducing the amount of insulation in walls, and using lower-quality materials. At the same time, lower-income families are often unable to afford housing built to higher standards. As a result, lower-income owners and renters often end up paying as much for energy as middle- or upper-income households, even though they are heating or cooling much smaller homes, and this expenditure corresponds to a much higher percentage of their income (Bernstein et al., 2000).

Fortunately, some innovative building practices can reduce the cost of higher-quality construction. To date, however, many of these innovations have not yet made it into the mainstream building market. The options in this section are designed to help bridge these gaps and foster the adoption of improved safety and efficiency technologies in the affordable-housing market. Specifically, the options provide financial incentives and arrangements that will encourage builders to develop safer, more durable, and more efficient homes, and that will make these improved homes more affordable to lower-income households through better mortgage terms, reduced insurance rates, reduced tax rates, lower transportation costs, and smaller utility bills.

Develop a Rating System for Housing That Exceeds Minimum Building Requirements

The state, possibly acting through the CDE discussed under "Develop the Capacity to Oversee, Coordinate, and Manage Affordable-Housing Rebuilding Efforts," can develop a system to encourage construction that exceeds minimum building requirements, such as a Mississippi Exemplary Housing Rating System. Essentially, this approach would begin with a set of basic minimum standards for building technologies and configurations, and then identify several categories of improvement above and beyond the minimum standards that would result in higher levels of safety, lower maintenance costs, reduced water and energy consumption, and reduced need for reliance upon the automobile. The improvement criteria could be based on findings from the recommendations under "Which Best Practices from Around the Country Can Be Applied in Mississippi?" The program could be modeled after the U.S. Green Building Council's Leadership in Energy and Environmental Design (LEED) rating system for commercial buildings, a program that awards silver, gold, and platinum ratings for buildings constructed to higher standards of sustainability, or it could be modeled after the EPA's ENERGY STAR® building program. This rating system would not be focused solely on energy use, however. Rather, it would more broadly encompass a range of factors that influence the long-term costs of owning and operating a home, including structural integrity, durability, energy and water efficiency, and access to nonautomotive modes of transport. Homeowners or developers of buildings that earn higher ratings would qualify for incentives, rebates, and other benefits. Specific incentive strategies are outlined in the following options.

Encourage the Federal National Mortgage Association Lender Partners to Offer a Combined Mortgage Product

The Federal National Mortgage Association (Fannie Mae) currently offers energy-efficient mortgages under one program and location-efficient mortgages under a separate trial program. Location-efficient mortgages are based on the idea that if a homeowner lives within a walkable neighborhood or close to public transit, then the individual's automobile-related expenses are lower, and he or she can afford to spend a higher portion of income on housing. Energy-efficient mortgage programs are similar: They assume that an energy-efficient home lowers energy expenses, enabling the borrower to use more income for housing. It may be possible for Fannie Mae to combine these mortgage programs and add a housing-durability component to create a single housing-efficiency mortgage product. Based on reducing the overall life-cycle cost of a home, this program could be designated as an experimental Katrina Recovery Mortgage. If a home were built to enhanced standards of durability, energy efficiency, water efficiency, and location efficiency, then homeowners would qualify for this product. Additionally, in contrast to Fannie Mae lender partners' existing products, Fannie Mae might consider the idea of qualifying homeowners for a lower interest rate or lower down-payment requirements (as opposed to qualifying a homeowner for a larger loan than one for which he or she would have otherwise qualified, which is the basis of the other programs). When the long-term operating cost of a home is reduced, the risk of default should be lower, so the rate on the mortgage could reflect this reduced risk. Downs (2003) and the Arizona Housing Commission (2002) discuss innovative mortgage options for affordable housing.

A pilot program would allow Fannie Mae to test the proposed financial mechanisms. They could coordinate with communities and institutions through the CDE discussed under "Develop the Capacity to Oversee, Coordinate, and Manage Affordable-Housing Rebuilding Efforts" to create one or more small-scale pilot efforts, which could be located in specially designated "innovative finance zones."

Encourage Private Lenders to Offer Innovative Mortgages

In conjunction with Fannie Mae, private mortgage companies may be encouraged to rethink how they offer mortgages to homeowners who live in homes that are efficient with respect to long-term maintenance needs, water usage, energy usage, and location. The rationale is the same as that for Fannie Mae: With reduced operational costs for home ownership, the risk of default is lower. Lenders could organize and carry out an independent study of the reduced risk of lower operating costs and then fold these reduced risks into their qualification and rate lending practices. The Mississippi Home Corporation or the state might be able to encourage banks to experiment with this option by providing guaranteed support, perhaps for a pilot period of five years, as the financial community monitors the program's performance. For instance, in the event of a default, the state could back the difference between the interest that would have been charged and the lower rate being offered under this program. This might be linked with the "Offer a Private Finance Initiative" option.

Encourage Insurers to Offer Innovative Insurance Programs

As insurance companies take stock of how they will operate across the Gulf Coast in future years, they can study the impact of housing that exceeds basic flood and wind safety codes and determine whether to offer reduced rates for housing that exceeds minimum standards, just as they offer reduced rates to safe drivers. To the extent that additional safety measures (e.g., elevating the house with higher foundations) reduce the risk of damage in the case of severe weather events, those savings should be passed along to homeowners. This, too, should help to make housing more affordable and create greater incentives for developers to exceed basic codes. The federal flood insurance program already offers reductions for basic safety features, but perhaps even larger insurance premium reductions could provide more incentives for additional safety strategies.

Offer Future Property Tax Rebates for Efficient Housing

With location- and resource-efficient housing, local governments will, over time, spend less on utilities and infrastructure such as roads and sewer lines. For this reason, they might consider offering reduced property taxes for units in high-density, mixed-use neighborhoods near transit, or for units that use energy and water at high levels of efficiency. Unfortunately, with the existing loss of the property tax base, local governments cannot offer such tax breaks at the present time. On the other hand, as rebuilding occurs and the local tax bases are restored, they may be able to offer future tax breaks beginning in a few years. By establishing such a program and identifying a specific date on which the discounted tax rate for homes with reduced infra-structure requirements would commence, municipalities can provide additional incentives for builders to create more resource- and location-efficient housing as the rebuilding efforts gain momentum. Ideas about how this program might be structured could be developed as part of the study discussed under "Which Best Practices from Around the Country Can Be Applied in Mississippi?" Neiman and Bush (2004) discuss several related tax-credit options in their paper on increasing the stock of affordable housing.

Create a Public Benefits Fund to Subsidize Better Construction

Several states have a public benefits fund to encourage energy efficiency in homes. In most cases, these programs involve a small fee on electricity bills, which the state collects and then redistributes to promote energy-use reduction strategies. For the most part, these fees have been uncontroversial because they are relatively small and the public recognizes the benefits of efforts to reduce energy costs. In Mississippi, this same approach might be leveraged to create a public benefits fund to support higher-quality, more efficient, affordable housing. For example, revenues could be raised from a small fee on utility bills, and the resulting funds could be used to subsidize developers who build housing that meets higher standards (higher ratings) or to back lower mortgage rates as described previously. Such an approach would effectively com-bine market-based incentives for higher-quality housing with government backing to acceler-ate the adoption process.

Options to Promote Local Involvement

One way or another, coastal Mississippi will slowly be rebuilt, either by large national develop-ment corporations or by smaller local construction companies. The local economy, however, will certainly benefit more if a larger portion of work is assigned to local firms. Toward this end, it may be appropriate to implement strategies that increase the ability of coastal residents and small businesses, including woman- and minority-owned firms, to take a greater role in the rebuilding process. At the same time, as the sheer magnitude of future redevelopment efforts will far exceed prior levels of construction activity within the state, it will also be necessary to enhance greatly the local capacity for building inspections. Finally, lower-income residents and affordable-housing advocates from specific communities can offer a wealth of information regarding local needs and circumstances, and they also have a clear stake in the outcome of affordable housing decisions. They should therefore play a significant role in the decisionmak-ing process. Collectively, the options in this section address all of these considerations.

Establish an Emerging Contractors Program

At present, there are many small contractors in the Mississippi Gulf Coast region with little experience in large-scale projects, and they will likely have a difficult time competing for con-tracts against larger, more established firms from outside the region. In order to enable Gulf Coast residents (including minority- and women-owned businesses) to take a more active role in the rebuilding process, it may be beneficial to develop a program for training local, qualified contractors to build high-quality, affordable housing. This near-term training effort would be designed to enhance the qualifications of local general contractors and to provide individual workers with basic construction skills. One element of the program would be to provide intensive, hands-on management training for small local contractors to develop their ability to bid successfully for government-backed projects. Another element would be an intensive program lasting several weeks to train local construction workers.

It would be logical to implement this concept at the state level, and the management for such a program might be provided by the CDE discussed under "Develop the Capability to Oversee, Coordinate, and Manage Affordable-Housing Rebuilding Efforts." There would also need to be branch training centers spread throughout different communities in the coastal region; these might be hosted by different universities across the state.

Increase the Local Capacity to Conduct Building Inspections

Because the number of housing units that need to be rebuilt over a short time span far exceeds the prior level of construction efforts within the state, more building code officials may be needed along the Gulf Coast region. Possible responses include the creation of a "lend an official" program over the short term in which code officials from other states and regions assist communities in coastal Mississippi, along with securing funding to hire and train new officials over the longer term. These steps may require efforts on the part of the state as well as local governments.

Ensure the Involvement of Affordable-Housing Stakeholders

Lower-income residents and local affordable-housing advocacy groups are likely to possess the best knowledge about local needs and conditions. At the same time, they have the most significant stake in the outcomes of affordable-housing policy and investment decisions. For these reasons, they could be granted the opportunity to participate in affordable-housing policy and investment decisions. One potential venue through which this participation could be channeled is the statewide CDE suggested under "Develop the Capability to Oversee, Coordinate, and Manage Affordable-Housing Rebuilding Efforts." For instance, requirements might be imposed to ensure that proposed affordable-housing projects have incorporated feedback from lower-income groups in the area prior to the disbursement of support funds, or the statewide CDE's board of advisors might reserve several of its seats for representatives from local affordable-housing groups.

CHAPTER FIVE

Summary and Conclusions

Even before Hurricane Katrina, the state of Mississippi faced considerable challenges in the area of affordable housing. With the extensive destruction wrought by the storm's intensity, these challenges have reached crisis proportions. To meet the needs of its residents and businesses alike, the state must now find a way to rebuild a considerable quantity of affordable-housing units quickly and to adopt strategies to make sure that the housing remains affordable over the long term.

Ideally, the federal government could play a strong, supportive role in these efforts. Recent trends in the funding and structuring of national affordable-housing and disaster-recovery programs, however, suggest that the response from the federal government will be insufficient to address the scope and scale of Mississippi's current affordable-housing challenges. As noted earlier, the total federal budget authority in inflation-adjusted dollars for traditional low-income housing program outlays has declined by almost 60 percent over the past three decades. In the wake of Hurricane Katrina, additional disaster-recovery funds from FEMA and SBA will certainly be available, but many of the recovery programs are geared toward property owners rather than renters. To make matters worse, FEMA and SBA recovery loans for homeowners are often restricted to individuals with a steady employment record and good credit history. As a result, neither low-income renters nor low-income home owners with spotty employment or credit records stand to benefit from many of the FEMA and SBA programs.

Given such considerations, one could certainly argue that a full response to the present housing crisis in Mississippi and other areas affected by Hurricane Katrina would include possible reforms in federal housing policy and spending levels. We do not dispute this point. However, the ideas presented in this paper are based on work performed on behalf of the Mississippi Governor's Commission on Recovery, Rebuilding, Renewal. Our analysis has thus focused primarily on policy options that could be implemented at the state or local level, or through cooperative efforts with nonprofit institutions and private industry. While the proposed options may not be sufficient to address the entirety of the housing crisis in Mississippi, we believe that they offer the potential to play a significant role.

In the prior chapter, we presented a variety of specific options for bolstering the supply and quality of affordable housing in coastal Mississippi during the rebuilding process. These policy options support different objectives, have different implementation time frames, and require involvement from different sets of actors. Table 5.1 and Figure 5.1 summarize these options and place them into a context in which they can be compared and contrasted.

Table 5.1
Assessment of the Importance, Timing, Goals, and Required Institutional Involvement for the Affordable-Housing Policy Options

Option	Assessment			Goals					Institutional Involvement — Government			Institutional Involvement — Private					Institutional Involvement — Nonprofit	
	Importance	Time Frame	Cost	Supply	Safety	Efficiency	Oversight	Local Involvement	Federal	State	Local	Utilities	Developers	Lenders	Insurers	Employers	Housing Corps	Other NGOs
Informing and overseeing long-term policy solutions																		
Three key analytic tasks	***ASAP		$	•	—	—	•	—	—	•	•	—	—	—	—	—	—	•
Oversight capacity	***ASAP		$$	•	•	•	•	•		•	—						—	
Increasing the supply and affordability of housing in the near term and long term																		
Permanent affordability goals	**	Near	$$	•		•	—		•	•		—				—	—	
State and local housing trust funds	***	Near	$$$	•		•			•	•								
Employer-based assistance	***	Near	$$$	•			•		•	•					•	—	
Developer requirements and incentives	***	Near	$$	•					—	•		•				—	
Dense, mixed-use zoning	**	ASAP	$	•		—			—	•		—				—	
Mixed-use public-private partnership HUD site pilot	**	Near	$$	•	—	—	•	—	•	•	•		•	•			•
Private finance initiative	**	Mid	$$	•		—			•	•	—		•	•		—	—
Subsidized mortgages	*	Mid	$$	•		—			•				•				
Community land trusts	***	Near	$$$	•	—	—	—	—	—	•		—				—	•	—
Nonprofit rental ownership	***	Near	$	•			—		—	—						•	

Table 5.1—Continued

| Option | Assessment | | | Goals | | | | | Institutional Involvement | | | | | | | | | |
| | Importance | Time Frame | Cost | Supply | Safety | Efficiency | Oversight | Local Involvement | Government | | | Private | | | | | Nonprofit | |
									Federal	State	Local	Utilities	Developers	Lenders	Insurers	Employers	Housing Corps	Other NGOs
Building safe and healthy affordable housing																		
Strict temporary codes	***	ASAP	$	—	•				—	•	•		—						—
Minimum long-term safety codes	***	Near	$$	—	•		—		—	•	•		—						—
Modular housing codes	*	Near	$	•	•	—	—		—		•		—						
Regulate shadow housing market	*	Long	$	—	•		•	—			•								
Prevention of inappropriate zoning	**	Long	$		•		—		—		•								
Increasing long-term affordability through lower life-cycle costs																		
Efficient housing certification program	**	Mid	$	—	—	•	•		—	•	—	—	—				•	—
Combined Fannie Mae mortgage	*	Mid	$	—	—	•			•	•				•				—
Innovative private lender mortgages	**	Mid	$	—	—	•			—	•				•				—
Innovative insurance programs	**	Mid	$	—	—	•				•	—				•			—
Future property tax efficiency rebates	*	Long	$$			•				—	•							
Public benefits fund	**	Mid	$$$	•	•	•				—	•							

Table 5.1—Continued

Option	Assessment			Goals					Institutional Involvement									
									Government			Private					Nonprofit	
	Importance	Time Frame	Cost	Supply	Safety	Efficiency	Oversight	Local Involvement	Federal	State	Local	Utilities	Developers	Lenders	Insurers	Employers	Housing Corps	Other NGOs
Promoting local involvement																		
Emerging contractors program	*	Mid	$$	—	—	—	•	•	•	•	•					—		—
Enhanced inspections capacity	***	Near	$$	•	•	—	•	•	•	•	•			—	—			
Involve local stakeholders	***	Near	$	—	—	—	•	•	•	•	•			—	—			

NOTE: * indicates moderate potential; *** indicates significant potential. $ indicates lower costs; $$$ indicates higher costs. • = primary goal; — = ancillary goal.

In Table 5.1, we first offer our assessment of the relative effectiveness or importance of the various options discussed. Next, we indicate the ideal time frame for initiating efforts on each option in order to maximize the resulting benefits. Some would need to be launched as quickly as possible, while others could be initiated in the near, middle, or longer terms. We also offer a rough estimate of the relative costs of the different options. We then show how these options support the different goals associated with the affordable housing rebuilding effort. These include the following:

- *Supply:* Increasing the quantity of affordable housing
- *Quality*: Increasing the safety of affordable housing supply
- *Affordability*: Lowering life-cycle costs related to maintenance, energy use, and water use to improve long-term affordability
- *Oversight*: Providing the necessary information and institutional capacity to manage and oversee the redevelopment of affordable housing effectively
- *Local involvement*: Fostering the opportunity for local communities, businesses, and residents to become more involved in the rebuilding process

Finally, we list the different types of entities that would need to play some role in implementing each of the options.

Figure 5.1
Notional Time Lines for Project Construction and Policy Options

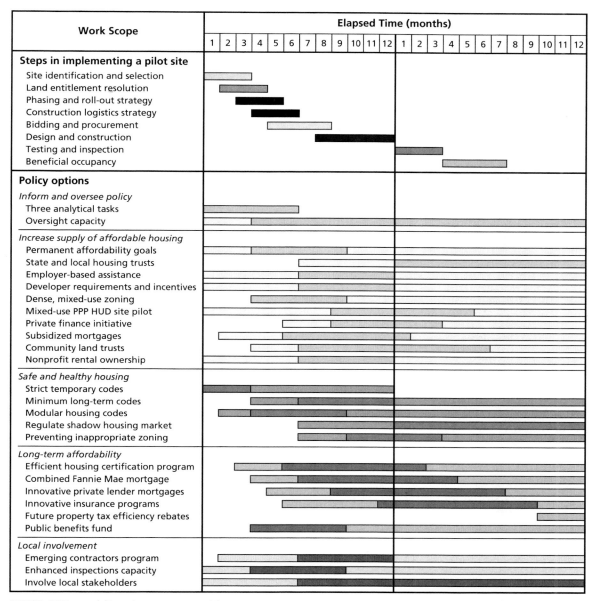

NOTE: PPP = public-private partnership.

Figure 5.1 offers a time-based perspective on the options. It depicts, in more detail, possible time lines for the tasks as they relate to the rebuilding of housing in Mississippi; in particular, it provides perspective on the appropriate sequencing of events for the smoothest and most efficient redevelopment of affordable housing possible. To provide additional context, the top section illustrates the time required to plan, finance, design, and construct a hypothetical large-scale affordable-housing project. Below this, we show the optimal time lines for the options presented in this paper. Within the figure, the darker portions of the lines represent the primary implementation phase, while the lighter portions represent initial planning before implementation as well as the longer-term operation and monitoring.

The process of rebuilding the areas in Mississippi devastated by Hurricane Katrina will be a difficult and complex undertaking. Rebuilding affordable housing, which is just one part of the problem, is no exception. As our analysis has demonstrated, some of the hardest-hit communities in Mississippi have high percentages of low-income people, many of whom lived in older buildings vulnerable to storm-related damages. As a result, the need for new affordable-housing options is likely to be particularly acute along the Gulf Coast. Unfortunately, evidence from prior natural disasters within the United States shows that it is very difficult—for reasons related to the limited financial means of lower-income families, the market incentives faced by lessors, and the structure of existing federal aid programs—to restore the stock of affordable housing to its former level in the wake of a major disaster. In Mississippi, however, there is compelling motivation to develop strategies for avoiding such problems. To begin with, providing a sufficient supply of high-quality affordable housing will provide tremendous and much-needed relief to the displaced residents of this area. Of equal importance, affordable housing will be critical to rebuilding the economy in coastal Mississippi. Quite simply, the communities will need workers to meet the state's goals for economic growth, and these workers will need housing.

Of the options presented in this report, several appear to be mission-critical, especially in light of the lessons learned from previous disasters. These include the following:

- *Developing better information* to inform policy
- *Creating the institutional capacity* to coordinate and manage the affordable-housing rebuilding efforts
- *Mitigating future problems* by requiring minimum safety building codes
- *Setting permanent affordability goals* so that a significant portion of workers can live in their communities
- *Increasing the supply and affordability of housing* by securing additional sources of funding and encouraging lower-rate mortgages, employer-based housing assistance, public-private partnerships, and modular home construction
- *Ensuring that the stock of affordable housing does not decline over the long run* by pursuing strategies such as community land trusts and nonprofit ownership of affordable rental units
- *Reducing long-term housing costs* by providing lower-rate mortgages for homes that achieve lower life-cycle costs through greater durability and efficiency.

The state of Mississippi and the cities and counties along the Gulf Coast have an opportunity to create dynamic, diverse, and economically strong communities. While providing adequate affordable housing for displaced citizens may not be the easiest task, it will likely be one of the most important. The options presented in this paper can help guide the efforts of policymakers and elected officials as they begin to rebuild the areas devastated by Hurricane

Katrina. To the extent that these options prove successful in the coastal communities, they may also be employed to reduce the affordable-housing gap in other areas of the Mississippi that were not affected by Katrina.

Details of the GIS Analysis

Our analysis first compiled information from the last complete census (2000) describing the characteristics of the residents of coastal Mississippi and their homes. Using GIS analytic methods, we estimated the effect of Katrina's flooding and coastal surge on these households and their homes. Our preliminary analysis focused on the three-county coastal area of Mississippi (i.e., Hancock, Harrison, and Jackson counties). This is not to say that other counties in Mississippi do not deserve attention.[1]

The Data

We compiled a variety of data using ArcGIS and Google Earth Pro. Pre-Katrina demographic and housing characteristics were drawn from the 2000 census conducted by the U.S. Census Bureau. Additional information included the national Land Use and Land Cover data for Mississippi from the U.S. Geological Survey. Polygon shape files were available from FEMA describing pre-Katrina FIRM[2] designations and SILs.[3] FEMA also provided post-Katrina, parcel-level inspection records (RSDE data) for homes in parts of Hancock and Harrison counties. High-resolution satellite imagery of post-Katrina conditions was available from the National Oceanic and Atmospheric Administration (NOAA).

---

[1] In the wake of Katrina, the Federal Emergency Management Agency (FEMA) listed 47 affected counties across Mississippi (and for which individual or household assistance was available [see FEMA, 2005a]), but the coastal areas sustained the most damage. Of the first 56 documented deaths in Louisiana, Mississippi, Alabama, and Florida, for example, 50 of them were in Harrison County (see O'Brien, Cooper, and Koch, 2005). Indeed, preliminary review of land cover of Mississippi suggested that most development was concentrated nearer the coast and where damages by Katrina were the greatest.

[2] "Flood insurance rate maps" are official maps of a community depicting zones prone to flooding hazards, including "100-year" and "500-year" flood zones. FIRMs are developed as part of the National Flood Insurance Program. For Mississippi, FIRM maps available as GIS data do not reflect events (including Hurricane Katrina) that have occurred in the last 25 years.

[3] The "surge inundation limit" (SIL) is an estimate of the inland extent of flooding caused by Hurricane Katrina's storm surge. They are available from FEMA as polygon shape files for use in GIS applications. They were created by mapping the coastal "high water mark" (HWM) elevations onto digital, prestorm, topographic contour data developed from recent Light Detecting and Ranging (LIDAR) surveys.

Unit of Analysis

The spatial unit of analysis for demographic information was the census block group,[4] which can vary in the number of people, households, and homes they enclose, and also vary in number across counties. There are 31, 131, and 104 census block groups in Hancock, Harrison, and Jackson counties, respectively, and there are between 600 and 3,000 people per census block group. There can be one or more people within a household, but typically a household includes fewer than 10 members. There can be one or more households within a housing unit. We have tabulated housing unit counts within block groups and subdivided these counts according to several measures and categories described below. Census block group limits do not span county boundaries, but they often span city boundaries. For this reason, the county-level results based on census block groups are likely more reliable than city-level results would be.

Measures and Categories

For each of the block groups, we categorized households according to indicators relevant to rebuilding and for which data are were readily available. The selected indicators illustrate the following:

- The extent of rebuilding that may be required, as indicated by the number of households and also the age of housing, which serves as proxy for the applicable building standard and potentially the durability of housing construction
- The financial means of affected households, as indicated by median household income
- The potential motivation of householders to share in the burden of rebuilding areas affected by Katrina, as indicated by whether damaged homes were owner-occupied or not. Our reasoning is that homeowners who lived in the homes they owned have greater motivation to rebuild them; whereas lessors may choose to invest elsewhere and tenants are free to move on to other rental opportunities.

We focused on four measures to describe pre-Katrina conditions of households and housing units: population density, median household income, housing tenure, and housing vintage.

- For *population density*, categories are separated at quartiles.[5]

---

[4] A census block group is a subdivision of a census tract and the smallest geographic unit for which the Census Bureau tabulates sample data.

[5] A quartile is a segment of a sample representing a sequential quarter (25 percent) of a sorted group. The first quartile represents the first quarter through the sample, the second quartile (or median) represents the first half of the sample, and so on.

- For *median household income* level, categories were separated at the FPL,[6] 150 percent of FPL,[7] and also at the median household income in the United States.[8]
- For *housing tenure*, categories were owner-occupied, rented, or vacant.
- For *housing vintage*, categories were separated at construction before and after 1980.

For all measures except for median household income, categories were mutually exclusive, and the sum of housing unit counts equaled 100 percent of the data represented by the measure. For household income, below FPL, below 150 percent FPL, and below U.S. median were cumulative counts, while housing unit counts above and below the U.S. median household income summed to 100 percent.

Overlay Analysis of Affected Areas

To assess Katrina's effect on households and housing according to these measures, we overlaid polygons of coastal surge (SIL) and flooding (FIRM, 100-year flood event) upon census block group polygons. The areal extent of enclosure by either the SIL or FIRM polygon then returned an estimate of the proportion of those block groups that were affected to some degree by Katrina. That proportion, when applied to the total housing-unit count for the block group, returned an estimated count of housing units that were affected by Katrina according to the above measures. The results of the SIL and FIRM overlay analysis are presented in Table A.1.

---

[6] According to the U.S. Department of Health and Human Services (DHHS), the 2005 federal poverty level, or FPL, was $19,350 for a family of four (DHHS, undated). In 2000, which is the date of data used in this analysis, FPL was $17,050 (DHHS, undated).

[7] One hundred and fifty percent FPL corresponds to the upper limit of eligibility for federal assistance through the Low Income Household Energy Assistance Program (LIHEAP), in which public assistance for residential energy costs and weatherization projects is available. State and local authorities have some discretion over specific eligibility requirements and how to allocate funds. More information on the LIHEAP program is available from FEMA and DHHS (DHHS, undated; FEMA, 2004). In 2000, 150 percent FPL corresponded to $25,575 for a family of four; in 2005, 150 percent FPL corresponded to $29,025 for a family of four.

[8] In the 2000 census, U.S. median income was $41,994 (based on 1999 tax returns).

Table A.1
Pre-Katrina Household and Housing Characteristics and Estimates of Katrina Damage Exposures

Area	Measures	Categories	Pre-Katrina Housing Units No.	%	Within SIL No.	%	Within FIRM No.	%	In SIL or FIRM No.	%
					Katrina Damage Exposure					
Three-county areas	Housing units	Total	152,386	100	75,733	50	40,137	26	81,491	53
	Median	<FPL	2,322	2	1,192	1	105	0	1,199	1
	Household income	<150% FPL	15,100	10	10,228	7	2,867	2	10,257	7
		<U.S. median	101,217	66	49,490	32	23,145	15	53,585	35
		>U.S. median	51,169	34	26,243	17	16,992	11	27,906	18
	Tenure	Owner-occupied	93,823	62	43,226	28	25,230	17	47,384	31
		Rental	42,288	28	22,454	15	9,459	6	23,613	15
		Vacant	16,275	11	10,052	7	5,444	4	10,445	7
	Housing vintage	Pre-1980	94,087	62	51,674	34	23,911	16	54,357	36
		Post-1980	58,299	38	24,059	16	16,226	11	27,134	18
Hancock County	Housing units	Total	21,072	100	15,277	72	8,293	39	15,706	75
	Median household income	<FPL	457	2	457	2	0	0	457	2
		<150% FPL	1,825	9	1,825	9	301	1	1,825	9
		<U.S. median	15,454	73	11,918	57	6,055	29	12,274	58
		>U.S. median	5,618	27	3,359	16	2,238	11	3,432	16
	Tenure	Owner-occupied	13,447	64	9,013	43	4,931	23	9,344	44
		Rental	3,450	16	2,856	14	1,181	6	2,901	14
		Vacant	4,175	20	3,408	16	2,180	10	3,453	16
	Housing vintage	Pre-1980	10,762	51	8,559	41	4,189	20	8,720	41
		Post-1980	10,310	49	6,718	32	4,104	19	6,986	33

Table A.1—Continued

| Area | Measures | Cate-gories | Pre-Katrina Housing Units | | Katrina Damage Exposure | | | | | |
| | | | | | Within SIL | | Within FIRM | | In SIL or FIRM | |
			No.	%	No.	%	No.	%	No.	%
Harrison County	Housing units	Total	79,636	100	31,051	39	17,445	22	34,399	43
	Median household income	<FPL	980	1	58	0	20	0	65	0
		<150% FPL	10,028	13	5,409	7	2,113	3	5,436	7
		<U.S. median	56,526	71	21,421	27	10,253	13	23,859	30
		>U.S. median	23,110	29	9,630	12	7,192	9	10,540	13
	Tenure	Owner-occupied	44,826	56	15,334	19	9,910	12	17,510	22
		Rental	26,712	34	11,554	15	5,440	7	12,469	16
		Vacant	8,098	10	4,161	5	2,102	3	4,407	6
	Housing vintage	Pre-1980	49,146	62	21,938	28	10,738	13	23,576	30
		Post-1980	30,490	38	9,113	11	6,707	8	10,823	14
Jackson County	Housing units	Total	51,678	100	29,405	57	14,399	28	31,386	61
	Median household income	<FPL	885	2	677	1	85	0	677	1
		<150% FPL	3,247	6	2,994	6	453	1	2,996	6
		<U.S. median	29,237	57	16,151	31	6,837	13	17,452	34
		>U.S. median	22,441	43	13,254	26	7,562	15	13,934	27
	Tenure	Owner-occupied	35,550	69	18,879	37	10,389	20	20,530	40
		Rental	12,126	23	8,044	16	2,838	5	8,243	16
		Vacant	4,002	8	2,483	5	1,162	2	2,585	5
	Housing vintage	Pre-1980	34,179	66	21,177	41	8,984	17	22,061	43
		Post-1980	17,499	34	8,228	16	5,415	10	9,325	18

Modeled Estimate of Level of Damage

RSDE data were used to model the level of damage in the peninsular area of Biloxi. Overall "percent damage" estimates for a sample of 2,629 points available for this area represented on-the-ground assessments by FEMA inspectors. These points were applied in a geostatistical algorithm called "kriging" which interpolates a surface between points. We then generated "equal damage contours" for this modeled surface, based on a kernel size of 350 feet. Overlaying these contour intervals upon satellite imagery acquired after Hurricane Katrina, we assessed the meaning of these damage levels by comparing them to FEMA's image-derived assessment of damages for coastal Mississippi. Categorizing RSDE "percent damage" as "<50 percent," "50–75 percent," ">75 percent," we determined approximations of FEMA's description of damages as "limited to moderate," "extensive," and "catastrophic" as follows:

- *Limited damage*: Solid structures sustain generally superficial damage (e.g., loss of tiles or roof shingles); some mobile homes and light structures are damaged or displaced.
- *Moderate damage*: Solid structures sustain exterior damage (e.g., missing roofs or roof segments); some mobile homes and light structures are destroyed, many are damaged or displaced.
- *Extensive damage*: Some solid structures are destroyed. Most sustain exterior and interior damage (e.g., roofs missing, interior walls exposed); most mobile homes and light structures are destroyed.
- *Catastrophic damage*: Most solid and all light mobile structures destroyed.

The results of our RSDE analysis are presented in Table A.2.

Table A.2
Pre-Katrina Household Characteristics and Modeled Damage Levels for Biloxi Peninsula Area

| | | Pre-Katrina Housing Units | | Katrina Damage Exposure | | | | Modeled Damage Levels | | | | | |
| | | | | In SIL | | In FIRM | | Limited to Moderate | | Extensive | | Catastrophic | |
Measures	Categories	No.	%	No.	%	No.	%	No.	%	No.	%	No.	%
Units	Total	6,404	100	5,546	87	2,381	37	1,236	19	2,295	36	2,839	44
Median household income	<FPL	0	0	0	0	0	0	0	0	0	0	0	0
	<150% FPL	2,957	46	2,932	46	1,430	22	347	5	825	13	1,754	27
	<U.S. median	6,018	94	5,226	82	2,201	34	1,152	18	2,092	33	2,742	43
	>U.S. median	386	6	320	5	180	3	84	1	203	3	97	2
Tenure	Owner-occupied	2,489	39	2,220	35	985	15	463	7	923	14	1,094	17
	Rental	2,901	45	2,437	38	1,008	16	586	9	1,049	16	1,252	20
	Vacant	1,014	16	892	14	390	6	187	3	326	5	493	8
Housing vintage	Pre-1980	5,779	90	5,005	78	2,129	33	1,107	17	2,093	33	2,553	40
	Post-1980	625	10	541	8	252	4	129	2	202	3	286	4

Error Analysis

We generally characterized the structures and households under pre-Katrina conditions according to the last complete census (2000). Owing to growth between 2000 and 2005, our approach does not account for new development or immigration of people to the Gulf region during this period,[9] and, for this reason, we have likely underestimated the number of households and homes that were affected by Katrina. More current data are available from the U.S. Census Bureau, but these revised data are estimates.

Block group data represents households and homes as uniformly distributed within the spatial extent of the block group, which in reality is not the case. Because households and homes appear to be clustered nearer the coast, for example, our approach likely underestimates the number of households and homes affected by Katrina's coastal surge.

SIL polygons are themselves modeled based on high water mark (HWM) and light detection and ranging (LIDAR) surveys and therefore may not always reflect the extent of surge inundation that actually occurred. SIL data do not account for wave height or wave run-up, while in coastal areas, FIRM data do account for these. On the other hand, FIRM polygons reflect 25-year-old estimates of the 100-year floodplain. Preliminary review of advisory base flood elevation (ABFE)[10] data suggested that flooding from Katrina likely affected areas well beyond the extent of the FIRM data used in our analysis.

Level of damage cannot be derived merely from the fact that structures occurred within FIRM or SIL boundaries, but it appears that greater damages occurred within these areas, especially nearer the coast.[11] Our analysis has not explicitly considered damage by winds.

In all, we have taken a conservative approach in our analysis, and in reporting our results, we have likely underestimated the number of housing units that were affected by Hurricane Katrina to some degree across the measures and categories we selected.

---

[9] According to the U.S. Census Bureau, population grew between 2000 and 2004 in Hancock, Harrison, and Jackson counties by 6.9 percent, 1.5 percent, and 3.1 percent respectively, outpacing statewide growth (2.0 percent). Population growth in the U.S. during that time was 3.3 percent. Housing units increased in Hancock, Harrison and Jackson counties between 2000 and 2002 by 6.1 percent, 5.0 percent, and 4.6 percent. During that same time, housing units increased by 2.9 percent statewide and nationwide.

[10] At the time this analysis was conducted, ABFE data were not available as polygon shape files; therefore we could not use this potentially more accurate dataset in our overlay analysis.

[11] Levels of damage are reflected in the attribute files for RSDE data, but these data are available only for homes in certain areas. Modeling damage levels by using RSDE data alone is limited to areas where a sufficient number of data points exist to create a modeled surface.

References

AHC. See Arizona Housing Commission.

Akintoye, Akintola, Matthias Beck, and Cliff Hardcastle, *Public-Private Partnerships: Managing Risks and Opportunities*, Oxford, U.K., and Malden, Mass.: Blackwell Science, 2003.

Arigoni, Danielle, *Affordable Housing and Smart Growth: Making the Connection*, Washington, D.C.: Smart Growth Network and National Neighborhood Coalition, 2001. Online at http://www.neighborhoodcoalition.org/pdfs/AH%20and%20SG.pdf (as of March 29, 2006).

Arizona Housing Commission, *Arizona Affordable Housing Profile: Findings and Conclusions 2002*, Phoenix, Ariz.: Arizona Housing Commission, Arizona Department of Housing, 2002. Online at http://www.housingaz.com/UPLOAD/profilech1_2.zip (as of March 28, 2006).

Bailey, Diane, Thomas Plenys, Gina M. Solomon, Todd R. Campbell, Gail Ruderman Feuer, Julie Masters, and Bella Tonkonogy, *Harboring Pollution: Strategies to Clean Up U.S. Ports*, New York, N.Y.: Natural Resources Defense Council, August 2004. Online at http://www.nrdc.org/air/pollution/ports/ports2.pdf (as of March 29, 2006).

Belsky, Eric S., *Where Will They Live? Metropolitan Dimensions of Affordable Housing Problem*, Cambridge, Mass.: Joint Center for Housing Studies, Graduate School of Design and John F. Kennedy School of Government, Harvard University, 2001.

Berke, Philip R., Jack Kartez, and Dennis Wenger, "Recovery After Disaster: Achieving Sustainable Development, Mitigation, and Equity," *Disasters*, Vol. 17, No. 2, June 1993, pp. 93–109.

Bernstein, Mark A., Robert Lempert, David S. Loughran, and David Santana-Ortiz, *The Public Benefit of California's Investments in Energy Efficiency*, Santa Monica, Calif.: RAND Corporation, MR-1212.0-CEC, 2000. Online at http://www.rand.org/pubs/monograph_reports/MR1212.0/ (as of March 29, 2006).

Blumenberg, E., "Transportation Costs and Economic Opportunity Among the Poor," *Access*, Vol. 23, 2003, pp. 40–41.

Bolin, Robert, and Lois Stanford, "The Northridge Earthquake: Community-Based Approaches to Unmet Recovery Needs," *Disasters*, Vol. 22, No. 1, 1998, pp. 21–38.

Brooks, Mary E., *A Workbook for Creating a Housing Trust Fund*, Washington, D.C.: Center for Community Change, July 1999. Online at http://www.communitychange.org/shared/publications/downloads/workbook.pdf (as of March 29, 2006).

———, *Housing Trust Fund Progress Report 2002: Local Responses to America's Housing Needs*, Frazier Park, Calif.: Housing Trust Fund Project, 2002.

Burton, Mark L., and Michael J. Hicks, *Hurricane Katrina: Preliminary Estimates of Commercial and Public Sector Damage*, Huntington, W. Va.: Marshall University Center for Business and Economic Research, September 2005. Online at http://www.marshall.edu/cber/research/katrina/Katrina-Estimates.pdf (as of March 29, 2006).

CB Richard Ellis, *The Hurricanes and Real Estate: Rebuilding After Devastation*, El Segundo, Calif.: CB Richard Ellis, October 2005. Online at http://www.cbre.com/NR/rdonlyres/A172E00E-6C06-405D-8AF8-76057E9F815C/284606/HurricanesWhitePaper_October2005.pdf (as of March 29, 2006).

Center for Community Change, "What Are Housing Trust Funds?" undated Web page. Online at http://www.communitychange.org/issues/housingtrustfunds/whatarehousingtf/ (as of March 29, 2006).

Chang, Stephanie E., and Scott B. Miles, "Resilient Community Recovery: Improving Recovery Through Comprehensive Modeling," in *Research Progress and Accomplishments 2001–2003*, Buffalo, N.Y.: Multidisciplinary Center for Earthquake Engineering Research, 2003, pp. 139–148. Online at http://mceer.buffalo.edu/publications/resaccom/03-SP01/10chang.pdf (as of March 28, 2006).

Comerio, Mary C., *Disaster Hits Home: New Policy for Urban Housing Recovery*, Berkeley, Calif.: University of California Press, 1998.

Deyle, Robert E., Charles C. Eadie, Jim Schwab, Richard A. Smith, and Kenneth C. Topping, *Planning for Post-Disaster Recovery and Reconstruction*, Chicago, Ill.: American Planning Association, PAS 483/484, September 2005.

DHHS. See U.S. Department of Health and Human Services.

DiMartino, Christina, "Picking Up the Pieces, Part II," *Waste Age*, Vol. 30, No. 12, December 1999, pp. 72–74, 76–79.

DiPasquale, Denise, "Why Don't We Know More About Housing Supply?" *Journal of Real Estate Finance and Economics*, Vol. 18, No. 1, January 1999, pp. 9–23.

Dobson, Martha, "UF Civil Engineers Find That Strict Building Codes Can Protect Homes from Storms," *The Florida Engineer*, October 1, 2004. Online at http://www.eng.ufl.edu/elinks/news/research/detail_article.php?id=350 (as of March 29, 2006).

Dolbeare, Cushing N., Irene Basloe Saraf, and Sheila Crowley, *Changing Priorities: The Federal Budget and Housing Assistance 1976–2005*, Washington, D.C.: The National Low Income Housing Coalition, October 2004. Online at http://www.nlihc.org/pubs/cp04/ChangingPriorities.pdf (as of March 29, 2006).

Downs, Anthony, "Growth Management, Smart Growth and Affordable Housing," Keynote Speech, Brookings Symposium on the Relationship Between Affordable Housing and Growth Management, May 29, 2003. Online at http://www.brookings.edu/views/speeches/downs/20030529_downs.htm (as of March 28, 2006).

England, Catherine, and Jeffrey R. Yousey, *Insuring Against Natural Disasters: Possibilities for Market-Based Reform*, June 1, 1998. Online at http://www.cei.org/pdf/1190.pdf (as of March 29, 2006).

Environmental Defense, "Clean Air Transportation Conformity: Accounting for Travel Growth to Assure Progress for Livable Communities and Healthy Air Quality," May 1, 2001. Online at http://www.environmentaldefense.org/documents/1209_TransportConformityBriefing.htm (as of April 12, 2006).

Environmental Systems Research Institute, ArcGIS 9.1, software.

Federal Emergency Management Agency, "FEMA Q3 Flood Data," undated(a). Online at http://www.esri.com/data/download/fema/index.html (as of March 29, 2006).

———, "Hurricane Katrina Flood Recovery Maps (Mississippi): Geographic Information Systems (GIS) Data," undated(b). Online at http://www.fema.gov/hazards/floods/recoverydata/katrina_ms_gis.shtm (as of March 29, 2006).

———, "Hurricane Katrina Flood Recovery (Mississippi)," undated(c). Online at http://www.fema.gov/hazards/floods/recoverydata/katrina_ms_mmds.shtm (as of March 29, 2006).

———, "Low Income Home Energy Assistance Program (LIHEAP)," October 23, 2004. Online at http://www.fema.gov/rrr/liheap.shtm (as of March 29, 2006).

———, "Designated Counties for Mississippi Hurricane Katrina," August 29, 2005a. Online at http://www.fema.gov/news/eventcounties.fema?id=4807 as of March 29, 2006.

———, "FEMA-1604-DR, Mississippi—Imagery Derived Assessment Mississippi Affected Population from Flooding as of 09/08/2005 18:00 EDT," September 8, 2005b. Online at http://www.gismaps.fema.gov/2005graphics/dr1604/rs_MS_Floodpop_090805_1800.pdf (as of March 29, 2006).

———, "DR1604, Mississippi," September 9, 2005c. Online at http://www.gismaps.fema.gov/2005pages/dr1604.shtm (as of March 29, 2006).

———, "More Than 50,000 Mississippians Housed in Travel Trailers," news release 1604-131, November 15, 2005d. Online at http://www.fema.gov/news/newsrelease.fema?id=20639 as of March 29, 2006.

———, "FEMA Flood Recovery Guidance: Questions and Answers About the Advisory Flood Elevations," March 21, 2006. Online at http://www.fema.gov/hazards/floods/recoverydata/katrina_la_qa_afe.shtm (as of March 29, 2006).

Feldman, Ron, *The Affordable Housing Shortage: Considering the Problem, Causes, and Solutions*, Minneapolis, Minn.: Federal Reserve Bank of Minneapolis, Banking and Policy Working Paper 02-2, August 2002. Online at http://woodrow.mpls.frb.fed.us/pubs/bsdpapers/housing.pdf (as of March 28, 2006).

FEMA. See Federal Emergency Management Agency.

Field, Charles G., "Building Consensus for Affordable Housing," *Housing Policy Debate*, Vol. 8, No. 4, 1997, pp. 801–832. Online at http://www.fanniemaefoundation.org/programs/hpd/pdf/hpd_0804_field.pdf (as of March 28, 2006).

Fischer, Will, and Barbara Sard, *Bringing Katrina's Poorest Victims Home: Targeted Federal Assistance Will Be Needed to Give Neediest Evacuees Option to Return to Their Hometowns*, Washington, D.C.: Center on Budget and Policy Priorities, November 3, 2005. Online at http://www.cbpp.org/11-2-05hous.pdf (as of March 29, 2006).

Google, Google Earth Pro, software.

Greene, Marjorie, "Housing Recovery and Reconstruction: Lessons from Recent Urban Earthquakes," *Proceedings: 3rd United States/Japan Workshop Urban Earthquake Hazard Reduction*, Earthquake

Engineering Research Institute, Publication No. 93-B, February 1993, pp. 11–15. Online at http://www.crid.or.cr/crid/cd_asentamientos_humanos/pdf/eng/doc3429/doc3429-contenido.pdf (as of March 28, 2006).

Hammitt, James K., *Residential Building Codes, Affordability, and Health Protection: A Risk-Tradeoff Approach*, Cambridge, Mass.: Joint Center for Housing Studies, Graduate School of Design and John F. Kennedy School of Government, Harvard University, 1999.

Harmon, Tasha, *Integrating Social Equity and Growth Management: Linking Community Land Trusts and Smart Growth*, Springfield, Mass.: The Institute for Community Economics, 2003. Online at http://content.knowledgeplex.org/kp2/cache/documents/98053.pdf (as of March 29, 2006).

HUD. See U.S. Department of Housing and Urban Development.

Hurricane Housing Working Group, *Recommendations to Assist in Florida's Long Term Housing Recovery Efforts*, Tallahassee, Fla.: Office of Lieutenant Governor Toni Jennings, February 18, 2005. Online at http://www.myflorida.com/myflorida/governorsoffice/Hurricane/pdfs/hhwg_report.pdf (as of March 29, 2006).

International Code Council, Building Officials and Code Administrators International, International Conference of Building Officials, and Southern Building Code Congress International, *International Building Code*, Falls Church, Va.: International Code Council, undated.

Jennings, Stephanie A., "Reinventing the Company Town: Employer-Assisted Housing in the 21st Century," *Housing Facts and Findings*, Vol. 2, No. 2, Summer 2000. Online at http://www.fanniemaefoundation.org/programs/hff/v2i2-company_town.shtml (as of March 29, 2006).

Katz, Bruce, Margery Austin Turner, Karen Destorel Brown, Mary Cunningham, and Noah Sawyer, *Rethinking Local Affordable Housing Strategies: Lessons from 70 Years of Policy and Practice*, Washington, D.C.: The Brookings Institution Center on Urban and Metropolitan Policy and The Urban Institute, December 2003. Online at http://www.brookings.edu/es/urban/knight/housingreview.pdf (as of March 29, 2006).

Kuban, Ron, and Heather MacKenzie-Carey, *Community-Wide Vulnerability and Capacity Assessment (CVCA)*, Ottawa, ON: Office of Critical Infrastructure Protection and Emergency Preparedness, 2001. Online at http://ww3.psepc-sppcc.gc.ca/research/resactivites/planPrep/Comm_Vuln_Assess/2000-D013_e.pdf (as of March 29, 2006).

Lindell, Michael K., and Carla S. Prater, "Assessing Community Impacts of Natural Disasters," *Natural Hazards Review*, Vol. 4, November 2003, pp. 176–185.

Lippiatt, Barbara C., *The BEES Model for Selecting Environmentally and Economically Balanced Building Products*, Gaithersburg, Md.: Building and Fire Research Laboratory, 1997. Online at http://fire.nist.gov/fire/firedocs/build97/PDF/b97102.pdf (as of March 29, 2006).

Listokin, David, and David Hattis, *Building Codes and Housing*, Washington, D.C.: HUD USER, April 2004. Online at http://www.huduser.org/rbc/pdf/Building_Codes.pdf (as of March 29, 2006).

Litman, Todd, *Smart Growth Reforms: Changing Planning, Regulatory, and Fiscal Practices to Support More Efficient Land Use*, Victoria, B.C.: Victoria Transport Policy Institute, November 25, 2005. Online at http://www.vtpi.org/smart_growth_reforms.pdf (as of March 29, 2006).

Loukaitou-Sideris, Anastasia, and Nabil M. Kamel, *Residential Recovery from the Northridge Earthquake: An Evaluation of Federal Assistance Programs*, Berkeley, Calif.: Policy Research Center, California Policy Research Center, 2004. Online at http://www.ucop.edu/cprc/eq%20recovery.pdf (as of March 28, 2006).

Luger, Michael I., and Kenneth M. Temkin, *Red Tape and Housing Costs: How Regulation Affects New Residential Development*, New Brunswick, N.J.: Center for Urban Policy Research, 2000.

May, Peter J., "Regulatory Implementation: Examining Barriers from Regulatory Processes," *Cityscape*, Vol. 8, No. 1, 2005, pp. 209–232. Online at http://www.huduser.org/periodicals/cityscpe/vol8num1/ch6.pdf (as of March 29, 2006).

May, Peter J., T. Jens Feeley, Robert Wood, and Raymond J. Burby, *Adoption and Enforcement of Earthquake Risk-Reduction Measures*, Berkeley, Calif.: Pacific Earthquake Engineering Research Center, PEER 1999/04, August 1999. Online at http://peer.berkeley.edu/Products/PEERReports/reports-1999/9904.pdf (as of March 29, 2006).

Morrow, Betty Hearn, "Identifying and Mapping Community Vulnerability," *Disasters*, Vol. 23, No. 1, March 1999, pp. 1–18.

National Low Income Housing Coalition, *Out of Reach*, Washington, D.C.: Low Income Housing Information Service, 2005. Online at http://www.nlihc.org/oor2005/ (as of March 28, 2006).

National Oceanic and Atmospheric Administration, "Hurricane Katrina Survey," September 9, 2005. Online at http://ngs.woc.noaa.gov/katrina/ (as of March 29, 2006).

NLIHC. See National Low Income Housing Coalition.

Neiman, Kimbra, and Malcolm Bush, *Increasing the Stock of Affordable Housing: The Value of Different Strategies in a Growing Crisis*, Chicago, Ill.: Woodstock Institute, 2004.

Nigg, Joanne M., "Disaster Recovery as a Social Process," in New Zealand Centre for Advanced Engineering, *Wellington After the 'Quake: The Challenge of Rebuilding Cities: Proceedings of a Conference Held in Wellington, New Zealand, 27–29 March 1995*, Wellington, N.Z.: Centre for Advanced Engineering, 1995, pp. 81–92.

O'Brien, Miles, Anderson Cooper, and Kathleen Koch, "Katrina Kills 50 in One Mississippi County," CNN.com, August 30, 2005, 1:52 a.m. EDT. Online at http://www.cnn.com/2005/WEATHER/08/29/hurricane.katrina/ (as of March 29, 2006).

Pender, Geoff, "Barbour Urges Stronger Building Codes for Public Safety," *The Sun Herald*, November 11, 2005, p. A5.

Peterson, Tom, "Community Land Trusts: An Introduction," *Planning Commissioners Journal*, Vol. 23, Summer 1996, pp. 10–12.

Petterson, Jeanine, *A Review of the Literature and Programs on Local Recovery from Disaster*, Boulder, Colo.: Natural Hazards Research and Applications Information Center, Working Paper 102, 1999. Online at http://www.colorado.edu/hazards/wp/wp102/wp102.html (as of March 28, 2006).

Phillips, Judith, *Housing Strategies for Mississippi: A Briefing Paper on Policy Issues Related to Housing Needs Within the State of Mississippi*, Mississippi State, Miss.: The John C. Stennis Institute of Government. 2005. Online at http://www.sips.org/Websites/Sipa/Documents/03385276-28e0-4f40-8980-f111ebd4a166.pdf as of March 28, 2006.

Public Entity Risk Institute, *Dealing with Disaster: Issues and Ideas Papers Presented During a PERI Internet Symposium*, October 1999. Online at http://www.riskinstitute.org/ptrdocs/dealingwithdis. pdf (as of March 29, 2006).

Schoch, Deborah, "Residents Fight Port Expansion," *The Greens of the San Joaquin*, 2004. Online at http://www.valleycleanair.com/news/story.aspx?ID=275 as of March 29, 2006.

Schwab, Jim, "Post-Disaster Zoning Opportunities," *Zoning News*, August 1998.

Shoup, Donald C., *The High Cost of Free Parking*, Chicago, Ill.: Planners Press, The American Planning Association, 2005.

Smith, Stanley K., and Christopher McCarty, "Demographic Effects of Natural Disasters: A Case Study of Hurricane Andrew," *Demography*, Vol. 33, No. 2, May 1996, pp. 265–275.

Southern Building Code Congress, *Southern Standard Building Code*, Birmingham, Ala.: Southern Building Code Congress, undated.

Spriggs, William E., coordinating author, "Principles and Priorities for Rebuilding New Orleans: Joint Statement by Black Social Scientists," *Viewpoints*, October 26, 2005. Online at http://www.epinet. org/webfeatures/viewpoints/rebuilding_new_orleans-statement.pdf (as of March 29, 2006).

Urban Land Institute, *A Rebuilding Strategy, New Orleans, LA: November 12–18, 2005, ULI—Urban Land Institute*, Washington D.C.: Urban Land Institute, 2005. Final version online at http://www. bringneworleansback.com/Portals/BringNewOrleansBack/Resources/Urban%20Planning%20 Final%20Report.pdf (as of March 29, 2006).

U.S. Census Bureau, "State and County QuickFacts," undated Web page. Online at http://quickfacts. census.gov/qfd/ (as of March 29, 2006).

———, *Census 2000 Summary File 1 (SF 1) 100-Percent Data*, Washington, D.C.: U.S. Census Bureau, 2000a. Online at http://factfinder.census.gov/servlet/DatasetMainPageServlet?_program=DEC&_ lang=en as of March 29, 2006.

———, *Census 2000 Summary File 3 (SF 3)—Sample Data*, Washington, D.C.: U.S. Census Bureau, 2000b. Online at http://factfinder.census.gov/servlet/DatasetMainPageServlet?_program=DEC&_ lang=en as of March 29, 2006.

U.S. Department of Commerce, *American Housing Survey*, Washington, D.C.: U.S. Department of Commerce, Bureau of the Census, Data User Services Division, 2003.

———, "BEARFACTS [Bureau of Economic Analysis Regional Economic Accounts]," April 27, 2005. Online at http://www.bea.gov/bea/regional/bearfacts/ (as of March 29, 2006).

U.S. Department of Health and Human Services, "Low Income Home Energy Assistance Program," undated Web page. Online at http://www.acf.hhs.gov/programs/liheap/ (as of March 29, 2006).

———, Office of the Assistant Secretary for Planning and Evaluation, "The 2000 HHS Poverty Guidelines: One Version of the [U.S.] Federal Poverty Measure," December 16, 2005. Online at http://aspe.hhs.gov/poverty/00poverty.htm (as of March 29, 2006).

U.S. Department of Homeland Security, "Emergencies and Disasters: Declared Disasters and Assistance," undated Web page. Online at http://www.dhs.gov/interweb/assetlibrary/katrina.htm (as of March 29, 2006).

U.S. Department of Housing and Urban Development, *"Not in My Back Yard": Removing Barriers to Affordable Housing: Report to President Bush and Secretary Kemp*, Washington, D.C.: U.S. Department of Housing and Urban Development, 1991.

U.S. Geological Survey, "Land Use and Land Cover (LULC)," February 1, 2006. Online at http://edc.usgs.gov/products/landcover/lulc.html (as of March 29, 2006).

Wisner, Benjamin, and John Adams, *Environmental Health in Emergencies and Disasters: A Practical Guide*, Geneva: World Health Organization, 2002. Online at http://www.crid.or.cr/digitalizacion/pdf/eng/doc14606/doc14606.htm (as of March 29, 2006).

Wu, Jie Ying, and Michael K. Lindell, "Housing Reconstruction After Two Major Earthquakes: The 1994 Northridge Earthquake in the United States and the 1999 Chi-Chi Earthquake in Taiwan," *Disasters*, Vol. 28, No. 1, 2004, pp. 63–81.

Yescombe, Edward, *Principles of Project Finance*, San Diego, Calif., and London: Academic, 2002.